THE *Experienced* HAND:

A Student Manual for Making the Most of an Internship

by

TIMOTHY STANTON
and KAMIL ALI

Sponsored by

The National Society for Internships and Experiential Education

SECOND EDITION

 CARROLL
PRESS
Publishers

43 Squantum St., Cranston, R. I. 02920

About the Authors –

TIMOTHY STANTON serves as Assistant Director and Coordinator of Action Research and Internships in the Public Service Center, Stanford University. From 1977 to 1985, he directed the Field and International Study Program of the New York State College of Human Ecology at Cornell University. Prior to entering higher education, he directed a community-based learning program in Marin County, California. He is a Past President of the Board of Directors of the National Society for Internships and Experiential Education.

KAMIL ALI was a rising junior at Princeton University when she initiated an internship at the National Society for Internships and Experiential Education. There she conceptualized and drafted this book for other students who want to be active learners. A leader in student government and Princeton's black radio station, Ms. Ali earned her B.A. degree in politics at Princeton and attended Harvard Law School.

About the Artists –

The cover design was created by Julius Spakevicius of Eurografica design studios in Boston, Mass.

Illustrations throughout the book are the work of Gordon Brooks whose drawings have enlivened other Carroll Press books. He is well-known to Cape Cod residents and visitors for his weekly cartoons in the *Cape Codder* and his line of silk-screened greeting cards which he designs and manufactures at his home shop in Brewster, Mass.

Library of Congress Cataloging in Publication Data

Stanton, Timothy
    The experienced hand.

    Bibliography: p.
    Includes index.
    1. Interns – United States – Handbooks, manuals, etc.
I. Ali, Kamil. II. National Society for Internships and Experiential Education. III. Title.
LC1059.S73   378'.103   81-24199
          ISBN 0-910328-33-X

Manufactured in the United States of America

CONTENTS

WHY THIS BOOK?

Mother always told you that "experience is the best teacher," and, as usual, Mother was right. Employers and academicians are increasingly tending to agree. While prestigious commissions line up to call for the integration of learning with working, internship and other field experience learning programs are springing up on campuses and in workplaces across the country and around the world. Despite the much heralded decline in student population, even greater numbers of teachers and students are moving their education out of classrooms and into the community.

This handbook is published in response to increasing interest. Written chiefly by students, it is intended to help other undergraduates or graduate students — (1) secure from the growing maze of opportunities an internship or field learning experience that is right for them; (2) make the most of this experience by linking it solidly to their goals for academic, career and/or personal growth; and (3) maximize the value of their work for organizations in which they serve as interns.

We thank these persons for their assistance in conceptualizing and editing: John Duley, Jane Kendall, Frank van Aalst, Deb Mann, Jasmine Adham and Randy Bishop. We thank Cheryl Ali, Roberta Heyward and Barbara Briggs for their help with graphics and typing of several drafts.

We welcome and would appreciate reactions to this publication by those who use it. Send your comments and inquiries to:

National Society for Internships and Experiential Education
3509 Haworth Drive, Suite 207
Raleigh, North Carolina 27609
Telephone: (919) 787-3263

1

WHAT IS AN INTERNSHIP?

There are many reasons for the proliferation of internship and field learning programs. In a time of declining economic indicators and budget cutbacks, employers in both the public and private sectors see student interns as fruitful and economical resources with which they can accomplish projects not otherwise possible. They see these interns as a way to inject new blood into old offices and recruit new personnel. Just as importantly, employers feel an increasing commitment to getting involved in the education of a new generation of workers.

At the same time, educators are rediscovering that experiential learning is an effective curricular tool, seeing it as perhaps the only way to maintain a commitment to the liberal arts and still adequately train students to take on responsible roles in a new and ever-changing society.

Students seek active, off-campus learning experiences for still different reasons. Some want to explore career ideas in order to get a step ahead in job hunting. Others want to take a break from 13 to 20 years of continuous and often passive classroom instruction, isolated from the so-called "real world" and carve out for themselves opportunities to shape their education and learn on their own. Others want to find a way to serve and influence a world they are inheriting and passing on.

But, what IS an internship? What is field learning? How is it different from work in general?

In this manual we use the term "internship" to mean any experience wherein students learn by taking on responsible roles as workers in organizations and observing and reflecting on what happens while they are there. Expected outcomes of such experiences include increased self-esteem and personal growth derived from successfully meeting new interpersonal and intellectual challenges, acquisition of particular skills and knowledge, exposure to various work roles and career choices, and service to a particular community or group.

Whatever the reasons for an employer's hosting a student, an academic institution's sponsorship of the experience, and student's participation as an intern, the key words are *planning, doing* and *reflecting.* Internships require students to take on roles of regular workers and observe the work environment and day-to-day experiences in order to interpret what goes on in both the external environment of the host organization and in the interior environment (personal reactions) of the intern.

1

Internship experiences are found in every sort of organization — non-profit agencies, corporations, government, policy institutes, neighborhood centers, etc. They are open to high school students, undergraduate and graduate students and continuing education students. They are part-time and full-time and may last for one or more academic terms, or a summer. They can be paid or unpaid.

Name an activity and there's probably a way for you to do an internship related to it! Information on how to find the internship opportunity most appropriate to your interests and abilities may be found in this book.

Here are a few examples:

- State legislatures sponsor students as legislative assistants in offices of state assemblymen and senators. Students work as receptionists and staff assistants. They research and write policy memoranda and they even draft legislation.

- Human service agencies seek student interns to administer or implement community service programs. Students of all ages provide counseling, tutoring, legal aid and a myriad of other services. They design and build recreation areas. They conceive and operate their own projects.

- Private companies recruit and place students in every aspect of their businesses. For example, a student may work alongside a personnel manager or conduct a market research survey or help staff a consumer affairs department.

- Labor unions utilize interns in organizing, lobbying and union administration activities.

Some Background

Experiential education is not a *new* idea — just a *good* idea that has been rediscovered. As the cobwebs are dusted away, the idea of integrating work and learning is regaining its usurped position in higher education.

Long before the creation of the first universities, "learning by doing" was about the only way to learn. The craft guilds and apprenticeship systems of earlier times are evidence that "learning by experience" was considered effective even then. However, with the creation of universities, a distinction began to evolve between vocational training and scholarly learning. Craft guilds were good for teaching practical skills but universities were the favored places for more cerebral endeavors. As the craft guild age gave way to the industrial revolution, this separation between experience and education grew stronger. Education, particularly in the liberal arts, became more and more theoretical and abstract, and further removed from the practicalities of life.

With the turn of the century, however, and the rise of specialized professional training, it became evident that preparation in certain areas of study required instruction and practice in real life or at least in simulated settings. Laboratory studies in the sciences, medical internships, and moot courts in law schools were found to be extremely useful if not necessary. A few pioneering liberal arts schools, such as Antioch, Beloit and Northeastern, motivated by the belief that even liberal learning was ineffective without direct linkage to practical experience, began to experiment with "co-op" experiences for their undergraduates. But it was not until recently that experience -based learning came into (or should we say returned to) its own.

Pushed by students' clamor for "relevance" in postsecondary education, colleges and universities began to experiment with incorporating off-campus experiences as general educational opportunities and exciting programs began to attract growing numbers of students. Research began to demonstrate the *educational* merits of this "new" mode of learning. Often begrudgingly, academic faculty climbed on the bandwagon.

As we enter the 80's, experience-based learning is growing exponentially while the rest of higher education begins to shrink. It is increasingly being regarded as one important response to the malaise of higher education, the problems of unemployed youth and a host of other social ills.

Some Definitions

With increased interest in field learning and internships coming from employers, government, educators and students, the lexicon which has grown up around them can be confusing to one just beginning to consider such an experience. Here are some definitions:

Service-Learning programs emphasize the contribution of useful services to an organization or community by students and the learning which occurs as a result of the experience, usually credited. Often these experiences are voluntary.

Cooperative Education students work and study often during alternative semesters, usually for pay. Some "parallel" co-op programs also offer part-time work and study simultaneously. Initially, these programs were found most frequently in technical fields and were popular among students majoring in business, engineering, and natural sciences. Now the term is used for a broader range of experiential programs in many fields.

Field Study and Practicums are labels given to academically credited field experiences designed to meet specific academic objectives. They may be general and interdisciplinary in nature or oriented toward specific pre-professional training. These experiences are often degree requirements.

Work-Study refers to the College Work-Study Program which has been a great financial boost for students interested in internships. Under this federally funded program, students with financial need receive work assignments on or off campus. If off campus, the government contributes 80 percent of the student's wages and the host organization, 20 percent. Students can work part-time during the school year and full-time during the summer. Thus, even if an internship is strictly volunteer with academic credit the only compensation, work-study funds may be a way for you to support yourself while you work and learn. If you are low on pocket money, check your eligibility with your college financial aid officer.

Why Do An Internship?

(1) *Employment.* With a tight economy and fewer jobs available, students with internship experience stand out in the job hunt. An internship can help you extricate yourself from the "can't get a job without experience, can't get experience without a job" double bind.

(2) *Take charge of your learning.* Internships are important opportunities for you to design your own learning curriculum and get away from the campus-based one which may be frustrating you. Decide what you want to learn, how you intend to learn it, and how you will evaluate it.

(3) *Theory into practice.* An internship experience can add more meaning to academic study by giving you the chance to apply theories learned in class to "real life" situations. Find out if the world as described in your sociology course really exists.

(4) *Awareness through increased community involvement.* You will develop an awareness of others' needs and a greater understanding of your role and potential contributions to society.

(5) *Personal growth.* Yes, you will grow from this experience. It won't transform you into a mature, responsible adult overnight, but having to solve problems in unfamiliar situations can bolster your self-confidence and show you where you need work.

(6) *Helping hand.* It is nice to help yourself but helping others increase their capacities is also a benefit and goal of an internship. Don't underestimate your potential contributions and the difference they can make.

(7) *New environment.* Introduce yourself to a new environment and the challenges and problems of a work setting. You'll also learn the meaning of teamwork.

(8) *Research.* It's an opportunity for experimentation and exploration of new and old academic and career interests.

(9) *Money.* You won't make a fortune but the amount you do make can help cover college expenses.

How to Use This Handbook

As you can see, internships come in all shapes and sizes, just as students do. Finding the one suited to your individual needs is not, therefore, a simple one-day search. Careful thought must be given to your own personal, academic and vocational objectives, your skills, your logistical needs, your financial situation and the academic requirements of the institution or faculty from whom you wish to earn credit. You will also have to find out where the internship programs or potential host organizations in your interest area are, who operates them and whom to contact in order to apply. Chapter Two should be helpful to you in completing these tasks.

Once you have secured an internship and you are on the job, you will need to insure that it is truly a learning experience or, better said, to insure that you know what it is you are learning and that what you are learning includes as much as possible what you intended to learn. Chapters Three and Four should assist you in this regard.

However, before setting out on your search for an internship, we recommend that you *read through the entire handbook.* The kinds of questions that come up during an internship can be equally helpful in finding the right one for you.

2

TEN STEPS TO AN INTERNSHIP

"My goal is this: Always to put myself in the place in which I am best able to serve — wherever my gifts find the best soil, the widest field of action. There is no other goal."*

STEP ONE: A Look At Yourself

Analyze your skills and interests; examine academic and career goals. What kind of experience do you want? What are your educational, career and personal goals? What kind of organization are you looking for? Work environment? Contribution? Define your limits — timetable for internship (how long? when to begin and end? part-time or full-time?), geographical limitations, paid or unpaid.

STEP TWO: Seek and Find — Gathering Information

Gather information from directories, guides, career services, intern office and other places.

STEP THREE: Narrowing Down — The Choices Get Smaller

Narrow down to organizations you want to pursue (10-20) making eliminations by organizations' requirements and personal considerations.

STEP FOUR: Making Contact

Contact your choices for more information about what they do, their intern program and admission requirements and procedures; and then make the first contact by phone or letter.

STEP FIVE: Choosing Your Target

Target in on a manageable number of organizations (5-10), make inquiries, plan resumes, arrange interviews and visits, continue to research and eliminate based on organization's capacity to provide the experience you want.

STEP SIX: Applications and The Waiting Game

Apply and wait; persist and follow up.

STEP SEVEN: Explore Academic Credit

STEP EIGHT: Offers — Your Final Decision

Select "The One" — accept and reject offers.

STEP NINE: Finalize Academic and Personal Arrangements

STEP TEN: Begin The Internship

---

*From *Journey to the East* by Herman Hesse. N.Y., Farrar, Strauss & Giroux, 1956.

Step One: A Look At Yourself

The first, and probably most important, step to an internship is to ana-lize carefully your personal, academic and career interests and skills and set your objectives for participating in an internship. Why go to all the trouble?

There are many methods for carrying out this self-analysis and goal-setting. There are several useful publications you can find in your campus library or store to help you. We recommend the following:

Bridging the Gap: A Learner's Guide to Transferable Skills by Paul Breen and Urban Whitaker. 1985. Available from The Learning Center, Box 27616, San Francisco, CA 94127.

The Complete Job Search Handbook: All the Skills You Need to Get Any Job and Have a Good Time Doing It by Howard E. Figler. 1979. Available from Rinehart and Winston, 383 Madison Ave., New York, NY 10017.

Resume Preparation Manual: A Step-by-Step Guide. Available from Catalyst, 14 East 60th St., New York, NY 10022.

What Color Is Your Parachute? by Richard N. Bolles. Revised edition, 1986. Available from Ten Speed Press, P.O. Box 7123, Berkeley, CA 94707.

The Resume Workbook: A Personal Career File for Job Applications by Carolyn F. Nutter. Fifth edition, 1978. Available from The Carroll Press, P.O. Box 8113, Cranston, R.I. 02920.

Career counselors and other persons on your campus will be delighted to be of assistance.

Exercise

The following is a list of items we think are crucial to consider in think-ing through your goals and objectives for an internship. Make "grocery lists" of your answers to each of the three headings. Don't censor yourself or eval-uate while you list *all* your answers. Then look over your lists, combine answers that go together, even personal and academic ones. Throw out any answers that no longer seem important.

• *List and evaluate your PERSONAL interests.* What do you like to do when no one is telling you what to do? What do you do for hobbies? Entertainment? What courses do you really like? What jobs or other experiences have had an impact on you? A clear picture of your per-sonal interests simplifies your search for an internship and helps en-sure that you get one worth investing your time in.

....

....

....

....

....

....

• *List and evaluate your ACADEMIC interests.* Why have you chosen your specific major? What puzzles you about your courses which an internship might help elucidate? What kind of experience could help you make better course choices on registration day? Many students find the campus a much more useful place once they have had an internship. Courses seem more relevant; they know why they are studying, as well as what they are studying. Think about your needs.

....

....

....

....

....

....

....

....

....

• *REFLECT on your career goals.* How do you want to spend your average work day in five years? One year? What skills or experience will you need? How will the internship fit into your academic and career plans? (Thoughts on careers should not be left for graduation day. Use an internship as a testing ground for academic and career decisions. Analyzing your goals now can help you find the right internship to test those goals.)

....

....

....

....

....

....

....

....

Now write for five minutes about why you want an internship. Don't stop writing during this period. When you are stuck and can't figure out what to say, write "I'm stuck. I can't figure out what to say."

....

....

....

....

....

....

....

....

....

....

....

....

....

....

....

....

....

These steps are all brain-loosening and data-gathering techniques. Now comes the analysis:

1. Go over your "forced writing" and circle all the key words — words that seem important to you. Define them to yourself. Be sure you know what they mean. Don't worry about anyone else.

2. List them. Then examine them for grouping, prioritizing and perhaps excluding if some seem redundant or no longer important.

....

....

....

....

....

....

3. Now rewrite your objective statement based on this second round of thinking and organizing.

....

....

....

....

....

....

....

....

....

4. Examine this statement for clarity to you. If you are not satisfied with your result, circle the key words again, pull them out, evaluate them and then rewrite again. Keep going until *you* are satisfied. By the end of this exercise, which can be very painstaking, you should not only be clear about what you want and why in relation to an internship, but you will also have the beginnings of a letter of application and/or petitions for academic credit which we will discuss later.

5. Try your statement out on other people — friends, relatives and professors. Do they understand it? If not, see if you can clarify some more.

Now that you have some objectives in mind, it's time to think more clearly about what sort of internship or work environment will help you attain them.

- *Make a checklist of personal criteria for the organization in which you wish to work.* What type of experience do you want? In what field? What kind of organization are you looking for? What should its style be? What kind of professional reputation should it have? Ask these questions and more to match your interests with the right organization.

....

....

....

....

....

- *Focus on your work values.* Which intrinsic and extrinsic rewards do you seek? What work do you feel needs to be done? How important is it to you to work as a member of a team? Do you like to work under supervision? Your work values and needs are useful as guidelines to determine what type of internship you want. Write them down.

....

....

....

....

....

Finally, consider the match that must be made between you and a particular internship project. What skills, attributes, abilities and limitations will you bring to an internship which will enable you to attain your objectives and be attractive and useful to the organization you work for?

- *Decide what you have to offer.* Even if you have had no formal work experience, you have acquired a number of skills — research and writing skills from term papers or management skills from student manager jobs. There are three already that you could add to your list of personal offerings. Analyze every nook and cranny to unearth skills you did not know you possessed. Be careful not to discard skills that *appear* useless. For example, a friendly attitude is useful in an internship that requires a lot of person-to-person contact. Sizing up your personal attributes is an extremely necessary starting point. Again, try listing them.

....

....

....

....

....

....

These lists will come in handy in everything from writing a resume and preparing for interviews to evaluating your experience when you've finished the internship.   After your self-evaluation, take into account personal considerations such as:

- *Geographical Location.* A governor's internship program in Alaska may sound good but is relocating to Alaska for a few months really feasible? Some programs with large corporations, government agencies and national organizations can place interns in branch offices across the country. If relocating is out of the question, check directories of internships that list programs by state. But remember – *any* organization is a potential site for your internship, not just those that have "intern programs." There are hundreds of possibilities within 100 miles of you right now. Ask yourself where you want to work and list your top locations.

....

....

....

....

- *Monetary Compensation.* Innovative students can develop their own projects and then persuade an organization to pay a small fee. Also, if you can prove that money is a necessity, you may be eligible for financial support from the College Work-Study Program. Another option is to check out your eligibility for stipends from sponsoring organizations. Practices vary widely from top wages to a fee for participation. Check out your needs and options in this area as soon as possible. List your estimated financial needs.

....

....

....

- *Duration.* Internships can last from a few weeks to a year or more. Longer internships *may* involve greater commitment than short-term ones (usually three to four months). Weigh the virtues of working part-time as opposed to 40 hours a week. Consider the degree of cooperation you will get from co-workers. Whether the internship is 40 hours or 15, it will be up to you to keep the internship from turning into "drudgery." How much responsibility will you have? How much time will be involved in your assignments?

- *Timing.* All programs do not run year round. Some are tailored only for the summer, others are in the fall. Some are not tailored at all. *You* design them in negotiations with a prospective supervisor. *Begin looking at organizations six to twelve months before you are ready to start work* and know *when* you want the internship. This is necessary to avoid missing deadlines as well as to plan your academic schedule so as not to miss required courses while you are away from school. When are you free to do an internship?

- *Academic Credit.* Interested in receiving credit? Research your department's requirements and the school's criteria for graduation. Don't be discouraged if your school has no established procedures for giving academic credit for internships. Attempt to show them the "error of their ways."

  A few people and places on campus to check about academic credit are:

  > ✓ Department offices
  > ✓ Academic advisors
  > ✓ Co-operative education, field study or intern offices
  > ✓ Individual professors

[Step Seven gives you more detailed assistance in this area.]

Step Two: Seek and Find — Gathering Information

To take advantage of their educational value, you have to know where to look for various intern programs. A treasure chest of opportunities awaits you if you look in the right places.

Written Resources

Written resources on internships can be found in your academic advisor's office, career services/placement centers, counseling centers and student employment and financial aid offices, department offices and the library. The following list of directories and guides provides a few information sources. There are many more.

Directories and Guides to Internships

Community Jobs Newsletter. Community Jobs, 1319 18th Street, N.W., Washington, DC 20036. Monthly newsletter announcing internships and employment opportunities in non-profit, social action organizations nationally.

Directory of Special Programs for Minority Group Members: Career Information Services, Employment Skills Banks, Financial Aid Resources. Garrett Park Press, P.O. Box 190F, Garrett Park, MD 20896. Includes programs offered by national and local organizations, federal agencies and individual colleges and universities. Revised every three or four years. Fourth edition, 1986, 348 pp., $22.50 prepaid.

Field Experience: Expand Your Options. John S. Duley, Editor. Instructional Media Center, Marketing Division, Michigan State University, East Lansing, MI 48824. Six do-it-yourself modules for problem-solving processes that aid in any aspect of an internship or other field experience. 1981, 50 pp., $5.50 (includes postage and handling).

Good Works: A Guide to Careers in Social Change. Joan Anzalone, Editor. Dembner Books, New York, NY. Assists students in finding internships or jobs in organizations involved in positive social change. 1985.

Integrating the Community and the Classroom: A Sampler of Post-secondary Courses. National Society for Internships and Experiential Education, 122 Saint Mary's Street, Raleigh, NC 27605. Provides samples of college courses with community-based learning activities. Useful for students and faculty arranging academic credit for learning through internships. Focus is on the social sciences and humanities courses. 1981, 256 pp., $17.00 prepaid, (includes postage and handling). $14.00 for current NSIEE members.

International Directory of Youth Internships. Council on International and Public Affairs, 777 United Nations Plaza, New York, NY 10017. Lists opportunities with the United Nations and its special agencies and non-governmental organizations.

Invest Yourself. Commission on Voluntary Service and Action, P.O. Box 117, New York, NY 10009. Describes service opportunities through internships with national and international organizations. Revised periodically. 1986 edition, $6.00 prepaid. (Make checks payable to CVSA/Invest Yourself.)

Journalism Scholarship Guide and Directory of College Journalism Programs. Dow Jones Newspaper Fund, P.O. Box 300, Princeton, NJ 08540. Contains information on various internships and scholarship programs for students interested in the field of journalism. 1986 edition; single copies are free; two or more copies, $2.00 each, prepaid.

Overseas Development Network's Opportunities Catalogue. Overseas Development Network, P.O. Box 1206, Stanford, CA 94305. A guide to internships, research, and employment with international development organizations.

The National Directory of Internships. Sally A. Migliore, Editor. National Society of Internships and Experiential Education, 3509 Haworth Drive, Raleigh, NC 27609. Provides complete descriptions of 1,000 selected internship opportunities across the country for students and adults of all ages. Divided by type of organization, including the arts, business and industry, communications, consumer concerns, education, environment, health, human services, government (all levels), international relations, museums and history, public interest, sciences and women's issues as well as local and national clearinghouses that make referrals for internships in all fields. Contains indexes by field of interest, by state, and by the name of the host organization. Revised every two years. 1987 edition, 350 pp., $17.00 prepaid (includes postage and handling), $14.00 for current NSIEE members.

State-Sponsored Internship Programs. National Society for Internships and Experiential Education, 122 Saint Mary's Street, Raleigh, NC 27605. Provides information about the internship opportunities offered by state governments across the country. For each program, includes the interns' responsibilities, number of opportunities available, educational goals of the program, eligibility criteria, application procedures, deadlines and compensation. 1986, 53 pp., $11.00 prepaid (includes postage and handling), $9.00 for current NSIEE members.

Student Guide to Mass Media Internships. Internship Research Group, Department of Journalism, Southwest Texas State University, San Marcos, TX 78666. Volume I lists print media opportunites; Volume II lists broadcast media. Revised annually. 1986 edition, $30.00 per volume or $50.00 per set with invoicing.

Volunteer! The Guide to Voluntary Service in the U.S. and Abroad. Published by the Council on International Educational Exchange and the Committee on Voluntary Service and Action through the Intercultural Press, Yarmouth, ME.

Whole World Handbook: A Student Guide to Work, Study and Travel Abroad. Council on International Educational Exchange, CISS Department, 205 E. 42nd Street, New York, NY 10017. Contains information on facilities and services for working or studying abroad. Organized by country. Revised annually. 1986 edition, $10.95 prepaid (includes postage and handling).

Career Services/Placement Centers

Campus Newspapers. Some internship programs advertise in student newspapers.

Newsletters and Bulletin Boards. Information about internships may be posted on the bulletin boards or printed in career newsletters.

Lists of Recruiters. Recruiters often interview for their organizations' summer and intern programs at the same time they are recruiting graduating seniors.

Work-Study Abroad Brochures. List work and study opportunities abroad for students interested in traveling for a semester or longer.

Other Written Resources

Library. Reference books on national associations, directories and registers of businesses list names and addresses to use for your inquiries about internships.

Association Publications. Many professional associations offer information on apprenticeship programs and other career aids for beginners. (Refer to such publications as *Career Guide to Professional Associations: A Directory of Organizations by Occupational Field* published by The Carroll Press, Cranston, R.I.)

Popular Magazines. The career sections of magazines can provide helpful tips on job opportunities and how to make the most of them.

Telephone Book. The yellow pages are always a good source for names and addresses of businesses and organizations you may want to contact.

Human Resources

On Campus

Fellow Students. From students who have done internships, you receive firsthand information about whom to contact, when to apply and what the internship is like. Ask around.

Internship, Field Experience, Experiential Learning, Career Development and Cooperative Education Offices. Tap these resources about special intern programs, application procedures and deadlines for financial aid or work/study programs.

Department Offices. Some departments sponsor intern programs that are open to students with any major. Be sure you are aware of field experience opportunities available through your own department.

Public Service, Community Service or Volunteer Service Centers. Most colleges and universities now have a center for community and public service opportunities, either in the Internship Office or as a separate center. These have information on opportunities for human service and community improvement right in your own campus back yard.

Your Academic Advisor. Ask him/her about fitting an internship into your academic program. He/she can refer you to the people and places that can help you find an internship.

Field Experience Learning, Career Development or Cooperative Education Office. Staff in these offices may be the most helpful ones in your quest for an internship. They also know the ropes and red tape procedures for arranging an academic credit for internships.

Off Campus

National Associations Concerned With Experiential Education Programs. Contact the National Society for Internships and Experiential Education for information on their directories of internship opportunities. Other associations will also have material on intern programs in their particular fields.

Departments of Education, Personnel, Community Affairs, Manpower. Federal, state and local departments have information on work experience programs. These departments in a particular organization may also be the places to get more information on internships.

Alumni Associations/Clubs. Many colleges organize their alumni to help students find internships, discuss career plans, etc. See your campus alumni affairs office.

Public Officials. The mayor, governor or other public officials may be willing to hire an intern, so contact their offices to find out. If you know individuals beyond the receptionist, call them first. Don't give up if you feel your first inquiry was ignored. A personal visit might get better results.

Public Interest Groups and Government Agencies (Federal, State and Local). Contact the local office and ask about intern programs. If they don't have interns, make anappointment to see someone to talk about developing an internship. Start with organizations that do something you care about.

Community-based Public/Community Service or Voluntary Action Center. These usually have the best listings on voluntary positions in human services or community action in the particular community. These positions can often be turned into internships with academic credit. If you wish to find such a position in a locale away from your campus, go to your library and find the telephone directory for that community and look up the name, address and telephone number for the volunteer center there. (Most communities have them.) Write or telephone for information.

From the telephone book to congressional offices, there is a vast amount of information about internships and sponsoring organizations and schools. It takes a persistent person to search out and use his/her discoveries. Once you have started uncovering programs, be sure to keep a personal file of who, what, when and where to refer back to in the future. You can lose an opportunity when you lose a name or address.

Step Three: Narrowing Down — The Choices Get Smaller

Now that you have unearthed a large number and variety of possibilities for your internship, you need to begin reducing your list of good ones to a manageable number (10-20) for further research. Sometimes students know exactly which ones these are and can prioritize them with no trouble. If you are one of these students, proceed at once to Step Four. Many students, however, find themselve in the situation of Tevye in *Fiddler on the Roof* — "On the one hand ... but on the other ..."

If this is your case, it is time to go back to the lists you made in Step One. What were your goals and objectives and how do these various internship possibilities relate to them? Which internship is least likely to help you fulfill your objectives? (Remember: If you find yourself attracted to an internship that does not match your stated objectives, it may be that your objectives are changing. Be careful when you narrow down the choices.)

Organizations' requirements also help eliminate internship programs for you. Certain internships may be off limits because of your age, year in school, major field of study or financial status.

Examples of off-limits programs

- A program that requires a senior when you are only a junior;

- An engineering firm that wants to hire a student majoring in a technical field, not a liberal arts major;

- A work-study internship or internship that provides a private stipend from an organization that requires the student to be financially needy.

However, if you are really interested in a particular program or organization, it doesn't hurt to ask anyway. You may have to talk with several individuals to find someone receptive to what you have to offer.

Weighing your personal objectives — academic and career goals, needs and requirements (location, duration, interests) — as well as the requirements of the organization should give you a manageable list to pursue. Use the space below to summarize your list of possible organizations.

....

....

....

....

....

....

....

Step Four: Making Contact

Having settled on a manageable number of internship programs to explore, you are now ready to make contact. The results from this step will enable you to narrow down the 10 - 20 possibilities to a smaller number.

Contact each organization in your large group to gather the information you need in order to do this paring down. Questions to consider include the following:

- Detailed information on the internship and organization.
- Admission procedures and requirements.
- Financial and residency requirements.
- Academic credit options, if any.
- Deadlines for application.

These inquiries can be made by letter or telephone. If you are nearby and have time, make an appointment with the appropriate person and go talk to him or her. If a particular organization does not have an official internship program but you still have serious reasons for wanting to intern with it, contact the personnel office and/or the individual who works in the area of interest to you. Ask if you could come and discuss the possibility. It is often useful before doing this to get a short letter of reference from a faculty member or experiential education director on university letterhead to help your inquiry receive someone's attention.

Many students find this inquiring and making contact part of the internship campaign particularly difficult. Some feel as if they are pushing themselves on someone who is not really interested. Others are simply shy about talking to strangers on the telephone. These are natural reactions and can be unsettling to deal with. Remember, however, that you are a consumer of an educational experience and you want it to be worth your time, energy and perhaps money. Just as when you make a major purchase, you want to be sure you have as much information as possible on which to base your choice. So, even if you don't feel very confident, try to remember all the assets you identified earlier which you have to offer. Remember that your labor may be going to someone for free (if your internship is unpaid), so get as much information as you can. As difficult as this stage can be, it is another crucial step to what can be the best educational experience of your life.

Step Five: Choosing Your Target

You now have to make some hard choices based on the piles of information you have amassed on a variety of internships. Which internships will be best for you? Who can really use your skills and time? From this large group of options, you need to pick a manageable number (5–10). You need to know about the structure of the organization, with whom or in what division you want to work. Use the suggestions in Step Three to complete this task. Your clear idea of your goals and objectives will be your guide in decision making. There is no other effective way to do it.

Step Six: Applications and the Waiting Game

Most internship programs require letters of application and resumes as part of the application process. These are your selling tools, so spend some time on them.

Letters of Application

Your resume and any application forms you have filled out need a personal introduction from you. That is the purpose of the letter of application. Large organizations may have to respond to you with form letters out of sheer necessity. You do not. A personal, imaginative letter introducing yourself, your interest in the program and your resume will help make a positive impression. A few tips:

1. Type your letter.

2. Address the letter to a particular person or department. It will save time if your inquiry reaches the right person who can help instead of getting lost in the shuffle of trivia mail. If you don't know whom to address, telephone the agency's executive director or company personnel office and find out.

3. Everyone needs some background information. As a college student, give your class and your major field of concentration.

4. Get to the point. What are your interests? Why? State your intentions and purposes in regard to the internship clearly. Describe how you expect to benefit from such an experience and what you have to contribute to the organization (skills, ability, energy, etc.). Ambiguity here defeats your purpose. Flowery phrases reflect an inability to be precise or confusion about your goals. The employer should be able to read this paragraph quickly and know what you want. Go back to your work in Step One for help.

5. Briefly explain points needing clarification or amplication in your resume.

6. Point out university sponsorship, credit, financial support or other endorsements you expect to receive or contract for in order to support your application and demonstrate the seriousness of your *educational* purposes.

Sample Letter of Inquiry

332 Olive Street
Susquehanna, NY 17078
July 23, 1982

Manager, Personnel Services
ABC Product Services, Inc.
839 34th Street
Busytown, USA 01234

Dear Sir or Madam:

I am writing to seek information on internship opportunities with your company's consumer affairs department during spring semester, 1983.

I am a junior at Trumansburg State College majoring in economics. Though I have no direct work experience in business, I feel that my academic and volunteer background well prepares me for a business internship. I have taken introductory courses in economics and seminars in marketing, personal finance and consumer decision making. I have also taken two psychology courses and volunteered for three summers as a YWCA camp counselor. During the Christmas holidays I help run the Susquehanna Family Service League's Annual Art and Craft Fair.

Now I wish to test my interests and skills in working with consumers and I feel that a business internship will be most appropriate to achieving my purpose. I am willing to take a semester away from my studies to gain this experience and I have the support of my college's field work office (see attached letter). I need not be paid.

Would you send me information on internships for undergraduate students at your company? I would like to know how your consumer affairs department functions and what roles student interns play in its operation. In addition, information on application procedures and deadlines and any transportation and insurance requirements would be very helpful.

Thank you very much. I look forward to hearing from you.

Sincerely,

Barbara Smith

Barbara Smith

cc. T. Jones, Director, Field Work Office
Trumansburg State College

7.   Ask for additional information. In order to decide whether this program is really for you, you may need still more facts about it. Ask for them. It is advisable to send a self-addressed, stamped envelope for the reply. *You* want the information, right?

The Resume

Your resume is the first impression an employer receives of you and it should be an accurate expression of your personal achievements and goals. It is your own work of art. A few hints:

1.   Type your resume.

2.   This is your personal ad. In a few imaginative words you have to be your own greatest fan and promote yourself.

3.   It is OK to be proud. A personal resume should express your pride in your talents and accomplishments.

4.   Brevity is preferable. Sell yourself on one short page. The employer wants a synopsis of your experiences, not your life story.

5.   Organize. The categories are up to you, but it is always best to have the information in order under specific headings (personal data, work experience, education, etc.).

6.   Add a personal touch. Standard resumes can be boring, so be innovative. Try something new or at least different such as rearranging the usual information. One resume may not fit the bill for every kind of organization — you may need more than one. You may want to use two or three different resumes in your initial search and then design individual ones for your final targets later.

7.   Go to your campus or placement office and get some help. Have a placement officer review your resume and help you spruce it up.

Basic Resume Samples

The following paragraphs and sample resumes on the next two pages have been reprinted with permission of Lynne M. Wiley, Director, Placement Office, New York State College of Human Ecology, Cornell University, Ithaca, N.Y.

The form is suitable for students seeking either internships or career employment. Although most resumes of this type need be no longer than a single page, more space may be needed to convey qualifications in human and/or social service fields. Use this form whenever work experience is fairly limited. Include a job qualifications statement or summary of experience immediately following the job objective desired.

The Redmond and Webster resumes arouse interest at once. Mary Redmond appears to be a young woman who is knowledgeable about the general area in which she would like to work. Her educational program has been planned with that objective in mind.

David Webster supports his interest in marketing by citing relevant courses. His use of the underscore lends focus and specificity to a variety of job-related skills.

Both candidates have used their time wisely and show evidence of commitment and ambition. Work experience is directly related to their job objectives. Volunteer time has been well spent. Extracurricular activities and family background contribute an extra dimension to these portraits. The resumes are patterned for easy readability with education taking precedence over business experience because of its greater importance at this career stage.

The total impact of these resumes is strong and positive. Much has been accomplished by both applicants at an early age, and the promise of future success is implicit in these brief sketches.

Example of a Basic Resume

———————————— MARY REDMOND ————————————

Box 95
Westford, New York 13488
(999) 555-1212

OBJECTIVE	Employment as a dietitian assistant in a hospital, health-care facility, or local community nutrition agency.
SUMMARY	A resourceful and self-reliant employee, experienced in working with both children and adults in a variety of settings, including business and education; motivated and compassionate; with a broad academic background; interested in furthering my education.
EDUCATION	CORNELL UNIVERSITY, Ithaca, New York Bachelor of Science, May 1980 Major: Nutrition

AREAS OF KNOWLEDGE

<u>Relevant Courses:</u>

Nutrition and Disease	Meal Management
Diet Formulation and Analysis	Adult Education
Consumer Law	Animal Science
Management of Human Resources	Food Science

WORK EXPERIENCE

Summer 1979	<u>Assistant, 4-H Youth Division</u>, Otsego County Cooperative Extension Service, Cooperstown, NY. Responsible for organizing all entries for Otsego County Fair and for the New York State Fair. Acted as chaperone for 20 adolescents during a visit to a local university. Transported exhibits; assisted in judging vegetables, herdsmenship, and 4-H workbooks.
Summer 1977	<u>Assistant Cook</u>, Vermont Girl Scout Council, S. Burlington, Vt. Assisted in the daily preparation of meals for an average of 40 people. Helped in the ordering and preparation of menus. Also assisted in clean up after meals.
Summers 1976, 1975	<u>Secretarial Assistant</u>, Huntington-Westford, Inc., Westford, NY. General reception duties, filing, typing.
Summer 1974	<u>Physical Therapy Assistant</u>, Fox Hospital, Oneonta, NY. Volunteer aide two afternoons per week. Helped patients with their exercises; transported them to and from their rooms.
	Was raised and worked all my life on our family's large dairy farm. Cooperated in carrying out daily chores.
EXTRACURRICULAR ACTIVITIES	Intramural Athletics Ecology Club Participated in Friends Program to orient new nutrition majors
HOBBIES	Jogging, needlepoint, racquetball, reading
REFERENCES	Will be furnished on request from: Cornell University, NYS College of Human Ecology, Placement Office, Ithaca, NY 14853. (607) 256-3170

Example of a Basic Resume

DAVID R. WEBSTER

226 Eddy Street   855 East Broadway
Ithaca, New York 14850   Long Beach, New York 11561
(607) 273-1251   (516) 889-9337

OBJECTIVE   A marketing-related position involving challenging assignments. Particular areas of interest include sales, promotion and market planning.

EDUCATION   CORNELL UNIVERSITY
Bachelor of Science in Consumer Economics (May 1980)

<u>Areas of Knowledge</u>

Marketing Management	Market Research
Advertising and Promotion	Consumer Behavior
Business Management	Accounting
Personnel	Micro Economics
Economics and Government	Macro Economics

WORK EXPERIENCE   TELEQUEST WATS SERVICE (October 1974 – August 1974). Long Beach, NY. Originally hired as telephone interviewer. Eventually assumed responsibility as <u>supervisor</u>. Involved <u>overseeing</u> the work of twenty employees per shift. Other duties included <u>hiring</u> and <u>training</u> new personnel; <u>briefing</u> interviewers on new projects; editing and tabbing completed work, reporting the progress of surveys and validations; preparing completed work for shipment.

CORNING GLASS WORKS (January 1979 – May 1979). Corning, NY. <u>Chosen</u> to represent Cornell University in semester internship. Involved in an independent marketing project aimed to increase consumer awareness. Prepared a <u>project definition</u>, literature search. Conducted surveys for primary data. Conclusions and recommendations have resulted in a <u>grant</u> from Corning Glass Works to Cornell University.

WORK/STUDY   OFFICE of RECORDS and SCHEDULING (September 1979 – Present) College of Human Ecology, Cornell University, Ithaca, NY. Involved with student scheduling and registration. Clerical documentation of official and confidential records.

EXTENSION MANAGEMENT INFORMATION SYSTEMS (EMIS) (September 1978 – December 1978). Ithaca, NY. Data processing.

PUBLIC SERVICE   Chamber of Commerce, City of Long Beach (December 1978). Santa Claus.

ACTIVITIES   <u>Ambassadors</u>. Elected to <u>Steering Committee</u> of Cornell University, College of Human Ecology Ambassadors. Assisting Academic Services and Admissions Office. <u>Coordinator</u> of Prospective Applicant program and High School visits.

Consumer Economics Department Council

Kappa Sigma Fraternity — Social Chairman, Spring 1979
Vice President, Fall 1978
Pledge President, Spring, 1977

INTERESTS   Tennis, Swimming and PEOPLE

REFERENCES   Furnished upon request

The Wait

There is no reason to rest and relax even after the last stamp is licked. Your resource file probably needs a facelift in preparation for replies from organizations and the nonstop flow of information from personal research. You may also be able to continue to ruminate on and eliminate prospective internships even without hearing from them.

During this nail-biting period, remember that the mail does take time. Organizations also have other responsibilities beyond processing student inquiries. Two to three weeks is the average waiting period.

Don't neglect to follow up. If the organization has not replied within a reasonable time (one month), write a second letter or telephone. In a second letter or phone call, include the name of the person you wrote to, date you wrote and the purpose of your letter. Be prepared to explain your interest over the telephone.

It is hard to say when or if you should stop trying because persistence often wins. How interested are you? The answer will tell you how long to stick with an unresponsive organization or how creative to be with one that is not encouraging initially.

Interviews

Many internship programs require interviews and you may receive such a request. If so, your resume and letter have been successful. Although an interview may not be the best method for assessing your abilities and potential contributions, this is the way it's done. There are things you can do to insure that you leave a favorable impression:

1. Make definite arrangements with the organization about the time, place and person who is going to interview you.

2. Collect your thoughts about your interests, skills, training and work experience. Keep a clear picture of yourself in mind. Use the lists you generated in Step One. Take a small notebook or cards with you to have the information handy for reference.

3. Read over the information you've collected about the organization. There's no need to pretend if you really have the knowledge.

4. If you are nervous, practice communicating with your mirror. It's OK to feel nervous, but a little practicing can bolster your self-confidence. Or find a friend and role play the interview.

5. Be neat and well-groomed. Appropriate attire for women is usually a dress or suit (skirt, jacket, blouse); for men it's the suit and tie ensemble.

6. Look the interviewer in the eye. Eye contact is essential as everyone likes attention. A slightly forward position also signals to the interviewer your interest. There's no need to hang onto every word but a nonchalant, laid-back position gives an impression of disinterest. Be relaxed but attentive.

7. Enthusiasm is always appreciated. Don't feign it. You'll be more transparent than you realize. If it's the internship you want, the feeling will be sincere. If it doesn't feel sincere, that's your cue to look elsewhere.

8. Put away your *ain'ts*. This is the time to leave slang at home and watch your English.

9. Most importantly, ask questions. There is a lot you *should* want to know about the organization, such as —

   - Duties and responsibilities of an intern.
   - Clarification of the organization's purpose and activities.
   - Type of intern projects.
   - Specifics — pay, time commitment, number of interns, etc. Remember: You are a consumer of this experience. The organization needs to sell itself to you, too. After all, if they are going to receive your services for little or no pay, they need to give you the kind of learning experience you want.

10. Express and discuss your interest in particular projects or tasks. Let the interviewer know what you would be interested in doing as an intern and how it will benefit the organization.

Points About YOU To Communicate During Your Internship Interview

- Why this particular internship is of interest to you. Communicate your enthusiasm.

- How does the internship relate to your course of study in college, career plans and other interests, etc.?

- How does your volunteer or work experience relate to the internship? How and what can you contribute to the agency or company sponsoring the internship?

- How will your college support your learning while you are working on the internship? How are credits allotted? What is required of your field supervisor and the internship organization?

- What is your time availability? When can you begin and when must you conclude the internship?

- What are your housing and financial needs, if any, while you are on the internship?

- What are your special concerns or questions about the internship which need to be answered through the interview?

Questions To Help You Find Out About A Potential Internship*

1. What type of organization is it exactly? (Public, private, nonprofit, etc.)

2. What would your tasks and duties be?

3. Does the site have a written job description of the position? (If not, consider helping the agency write one.) What day-to-day assignments can you expect?

4. Does the position require any special skills, experience or education?

5. What hours would you be working?

6. Who would be your immediate supervisor and how closely would you be supervised? (Ask to meet this person on your first visit before you agree to volunteer.)

7. How were the needs of those being served initially identified and how does the agency stay in touch with clients to determine if the service is meeting those needs?

8. Where does the department in which you will be assigned fit into the overall structure of the organization?

9. Is orientation provided for interns? By whom? What is the content of the orientation? What are its goals?

10. Is the internship one that might place you in the situation of handling an emergency? If so, what training will you be given for such a situation?

11. Are you personally liable for any accidents that might occur through the performance of your duties? How does the law stand on this? (This might take some effort to find out.)

12. Does the site have insurance covering interns? If so, how extensive is it? Are health, personal liability and automobile liability (if you would be driving as part of your job) all covered in the site's insurance plan? If not, what kind of insurance coverage does the site recommend for you?

13. Are you likely to incur any expenses in the performance of your duties? Will you be reimbursed?

14. Are there any special rules you should know about? (This is important because it could affect your work and/or happiness on the site.)

15. Does the site offer any special privileges or benefits to its interns?

16. What is the general role and status of interns at the site?

17. Are there any laws or legal limitations which apply to you because of your work at the site? (Bonding procedures, for example, or confidentiality or security clearance.)

18. Can the agency or company assist you in finding housing while in the internship?

From the interview, the organization should be able to gain a picture of what your abilities are and how they can use your talents. *You* should come away with an idea of what the internship will require from you and a glimpse of what your supervisor will be like. Can you work with him/her? The interview provides a chance for you and the organization to feel out the situation and avoid problems later. It is another important opportunity for you to figure out what you want and which opportunity can provide it.

---

* Adapted from *Service-Learning: A guide for college students.* National Center for Service-Learning/ ACTION, p. 24.

Step Seven: Explore Academic Credit

If you are interested in earning academic credit for your internship, the period when you await your responses to your internship applications is a good time to explore the options if you have not done so already.

Since each campus has its own requirements and regulations for crediting field experience learning, it is difficult to give a great deal of specific assistance in this manual. You will have to be your own sleuth. However, there are a few general things you can do which should prove useful on any campus:

1. *Find out the credit-granting procedures that are relevant to your learning objectives and internship possibilities.*

    Often the best informational resource to start with is students who have done internships and earned credit on your campus. Find out how they set up their credit arrangements and which faculty members, departments or offices were most helpful and supportive.

    Contact the campus centers for experiential learning if they exist on your campus. Off-campus learning, career development and cooperative education offices often supervise student interns. If you seek credit from an academic department and your campus has no central experiential learning office, talk to undergraduate advising coordinators in departments that have a reputation for encouraging field work (psychology, political science, etc.). Ask your own advisor.

2. *Match the available credit-granting options with the nature of the internships to which you have applied and the kinds of credit you need to earn.*

    •   Which option for earning credit is best for you in terms of the kind of academic supervision you want for your internship? If you think you will be working in some sort of business or corporation, do you want a business administration professor to help you sort it out? A psychologist? Or an economist? The answer will depend on what you expect to be doing on your internship and what kind of help you want from your home campus.

    •   Which option leaves you with credits you can really use in your major or elective requirement areas? If you want some or all of your credits to go toward fulfilling your major degree requirements and you think your internship experience will have direct relevance to your major discipline area(s), talk to your advisor and concentrate on obtaining academic sponsorship for your internship from your major department.

    Don't be bashful. Even English and history departments sometimes grant credit for internships if the learning that results from the internship can be described as "English" or "history." Find a faculty member who is interested in you and your internship and be creative!

    •   Finally, if an internship program to which you have applied grants credit through another institution, find out if you can simply transfer the credit to your home campus. Some of it may be applicable to your major. You could then register "in absentia" if your campus allows you to and possibly save yourself some tuition money.

    Be sure to check out *all* of your options with someone on your campus who knows what you intend to do and how best to navigate your college's maze of red tape.

Finding answers to the questions that arise when you consider which way to credit your internship may be complicated or simple depending on your campus and its attitudes toward field experience learning, your curricular requirements and the nature of your internship. However, seek them out *now*. Trying to patch together credit programs for an internship once you are working away from campus can be difficult if not impossible. Organizing your academic supervision now, even before you have actually obtained an internship, will save you headaches later on.

3. *Get acquainted with the faculty and staff with whom you choose to make your credit arrangements.*

Introduce yourself, your interest and objectives for doing an internship and describe to your potential faculty sponsor* the programs to which you have applied. Learn from him/her the exact procedures and requirements you must follow to earn the credit. What reading and writing is involved? How will your internship organization supervisor have to be involved? What will your faculty sponsor expect of you, your work supervisor, your internship program, etc.?

A word of advice: Faculty members are sometimes reluctant to sponsor students in internships because such supervision is extra work for them for which they receive little reward. In addition, they may not know exactly what is involved in sponsoring student internships for credit or for what they are responsible. Thus, they shy away from involvement.

If you must acquire a faculty sponsor to credit your internship, prepare yourself for this possible reluctance before you approach him/her in the following ways:

• Find out from field experience learning offices, departmental secretaries or advisors what your college or department will expect your faculty sponsor to do. If there are policies and procedures that govern sponsorship and crediting of internships at your college, you may have to tell your faculty sponsor what they are.

• Write up a short outline or summary statement itemizing your intentions, including —

  ▫ Your academic objectives — what you want to learn. (Go back to Step One for help on this.)

  ▫ The nature of the assistance, supervision and evaluation which you want from your faculty sponsor.

    What kind of help do you think you might want once you are away from campus? What *kind* of assistance can this particular faculty sponsor give you? What *kind* and amount of reading and writing do you want him/her to assign you? How and by whom do you wish to be evaluated?

For assistance in thinking through the above, turn to Chapter Three, the section on Learning Tips, and to Chapter Four the section on Reflections on an Internship/Summing It Up. You will find many ideas which you and your sponsor can utilize in your academic supervision program.

---

* The term "faculty sponsor" as used in this manual refers generally to anyone on the staff of your college or university (faculty member, counselor, administrator, etc.) who is responsible for advising and supervising students throughout an internship and sponsoring the experience for credit.

Be reasonable. Think about the policies and requirements that govern granting academic credit on your campus, what you want to do and the amount of time you and your faculty sponsor will have, etc., in making your suggestions.

Writing such a statement will not only help you think through what you want to say to your faculty sponsor. It will also give you a headstart on writing a learning contract for your internship if one is required. See Chapter Three for an example of a learning contract.

- Make an appointment with the faculty member you have chosen. Take your statement (one copy for you and one for him/her) and talk it over. Explain your objectives, describe the internships to which you have applied. State your need and desire for credit and discuss potential supervision arrangements.

Try to stay relaxed. Even though talking to professors can sometimes be intimidating, you are only inviting his/her involvement at this time and suggesting tentative arrangements. There is no need or expectation for you to know exactly what you want in the way of supervision. Your objective is simply to interest a faculty member in working with you and get him/her to agree to sponsor your internship for credit. Detailed arrangements, writing learning contracts, etc., should be made once you have been accepted into and committed yourself to a particular internship.

Presenting your potential academic sponsor such an organized statement, talking to him/her in a way that suggests that you are serious about the learning aspects of your internship and indicating that you do not intend to be totally dependent on him/her for arranging the nature of the supervision should attract a faculty member to working with you and granting you credit and establishing a good working relationship. You will discover that faculty are much more eager to sponsor your internship when you take responsibility for your learning in this way. You will feel better, too!

4. *Having identified the credit option which best meets your needs, note any requirements or expectations you and your faculty sponsor have for supervision of your potential internship.*

When you begin to receive responses to your internship applications, you may be asked for information; so have it at hand. If you are not asked, once you have your internship, be sure to let your internship supervisor* know how he/she will be expected to participate in your academic credit arrangements. He/she will not react well if you surprise him/her at the end of your internship by requesting a lengthy and detailed final evaluation. (See pages 76-80 for an example of an evaluation form.)

Step Eight: Offers — Your Final Decision

Not every organization can have you! You may have to make a decision between the interesting internship and the one that excites you. These few pointers may help you in your selection:

1. Which organization fits your personal interests and needs the best?

2. Are your abilities suited to the organization?

3. How did you get along with your supervisor in the initial interview?

---

* The term "internship supervisor" as used in this manual refers generally to the person in your internship organization who is primarily responsible for supervising your work activities.

4. Consider the general work atmosphere — employee relations, dress, etc.

5. How much responsibility will you have?

6. How well does the project/assignments relate to your career goals? Academic goals?

7. Is the project worthwhile? How will it help the community? Who is going to benefit from the work you do?

8. Compare the possible academic benefits of each internship. What can you learn? How will you know if you learned it?

Accepting/Rejecting

When you start receiving offers, things can get hectic and delicate. If you have followed through on several applications, you must be careful in your acceptance or rejection of offers.

Think carefully about your interest in particular internships. Be sure that you not only *want* to do but are *able* to do it. Once you say "yes" you have made a commitment and a lot of people depend on you to follow through. Pulling out later because a "better" internship comes along can have a considerably negative impact on your reputation. You need to be mindful of the amount of work and care that the organization's staff has had to put into planning your internship, the consequences for these staff members if you withdraw and the effect your withdrawal may have on the organization's attitude toward future student applicants. So be careful, thoughtful, sensitive and diplomatic. If you find yourself having to accept or reject one internship before you hear about another, be open and honest. Tell the people with the deadline your dilemma and ask for an extension. You and they will both be better off in the end.

Once you decide which internship is for you, send that organization a typed acceptance letter and be sure to clear the air about —

1. *Pay Arrangements.* Some programs have deadlines for pay contracts which must be signed and returned to the school by a specific date.

2. *Work Schedule.* Internships for academic credit have strict hour requirements. Inform the organization about when you are going to begin and end the internship. You may not want to start work immediately, so let your supervisor know this. They are human and can understand your needing a break after classes. If you do not begin work immediately, you can use the time to finish up everything you may have left hanging while making your decision.

3. *Job Duties and the Purpose of Your Personal Project.* The organization or school may need a written project proposal.

4. *Your Intern Supervisor.* You need to know the name of the person to whom you will be directly responsible.

5. *Academic Sponsor.* If you have made academic credit arrangements by this time and know the name of your faculty sponsor, supply the internship organization with this person's name, address, telephone number, etc., and outline any requirements this person may ask of the internship placement organization, such as visits, evaluation forms, etc.

Show Appreciation

Whether you reject an internship offer or are rejected by them, it helps to send a brief thank-you letter. It will be appreciated. Don't hesitate to ask why you were turned down. If you don't, you have missed a chance for potentially important feedback on your skills, your self-presentation or the way the application process worked. Who knows, you may get advice or contacts for other opportunities.

Sample letters of all these negotiations are given at the end of this chapter.

Step Nine: Finalizing Academic and Personal Arrangements

Academic

If you are intending to earn academic credit for your internship, you must usually finalize arrangements with your faculty sponsor before you leave campus.

Learning Contracts

Be sure *everyone* (you, your academic sponsor and your internship supervisor) is aware of and agrees to the academic supervision procedures you have devised and work activities you intend to undertake. If you have not done so already, we suggest you write them down in a *Learning Contract.* Ask your faculty sponsor and internship supervisor to add their own ideas, sign it and give them all copies. (See the section on *Learning Contracts* in Chapter Three for assistance in drawing one up. Give yourself time to do this. It can be a complicated process involving some sensitive negotiations.)

Tuition/Registration.

Be certain you know how, when and with whom to register for your credit. Let your university registrar's office know what your off-campus address will be while you are on your internship. If you don't know it yet, find out to whom to send your address when you have one.

Completing these arrangements can become a real burden if left until after you leave campus. Do them *now!*

Personal — Housing

If the internship includes relocating, finalize your arrangements *before* you leave school. New York City or the District of Columbia, for example, are very expensive places to live and apartments are scarce. Therefore, if you haven't already done so, put a note on the student union or career services bulletin board for a roommate to share expenses. Finding a place to live is a big problem when you are unfamiliar with the area and the neighborhoods. A few places to check for housing tips are:

Bulletin Boards

Student Union. Other interns will be looking for roommates and probably posting notices in visible places on campus such as the student union.

Career Services/Intern Coordinators/Department Offices. The person running the internship program may be coordinating living arrangements for their interns, so check here to find out about housing.

College Friends

If you have friends or relatives who live in the area, you should check with them about staying for the duration of the internship. These arrangements are a little easier on your pocketbook. If you don't stay with friends, they can still refer you to good neighborhoods.

Alumni Club

Here again, alumni in your internship area can be useful in your househunting. Check to see if someone wants a house looked after. Ask to be referred to any possible housing availabilities.

Universities in the Area

During the summer, dormitories are often empty and less expensive to rent than apartments or furnished rooms. In a city with many universities, there may be a formal intern housing program complete with meal plans.

Local Drugstores

Many times drugstores will have information booklets on apartments which are very helpful.

The Internship Organization

Your supervisor may have a few tips on housing if the organization has had interns in the past. Ask, just in case.

Classified Ads

Try to purchase a local newspaper to check out the housing ads. House-sitting arrangements are sometimes advertised and usually cheaper than renting an apartment. Put your own ad in.

Pick up a couple of brochures on the place or talk to people at school from the area. They can provide "survival" hints that won't be found in any tourist guide.

Health Insurance

Most universities offer supplemental health insurance policies to help students pay for medical treatment not obtained at a campus health clinic. Since you will be away from campus, you will not have access to such a clinic and thus will be responsible for any and all medical expenses you may incur. For this reason it is important that you continue your university medical insurance coverage, if you have it, or consider other means of insuring your ability to provide yourself health care while on your internship.

Check with your college or university health insurance office to be sure their policy covers you while you are away from campus, if you have such a policy. If not, consult with your family to be sure you know how you will obtain health services if they should be needed.

Step Ten: Begin the Internship!

BRIEF DESCRIPTION of an INTERNSHIP SEARCH
by Jasmine Adham

Since I was interested in living in the Washington area for my semester off campus, I used that as my starting point in looking for an internship. Where I would live was an important consideration for me — I come from a small up-state New York town and this would be my first time living in a major metropolitan city. New York City was definitely out of the question and I had visited Washington and liked it and had friends there. A new working environment is made easier if one doesn't also have to worry about living situations.

I thought about what I wanted to do and to accomplish which was to find out how I could apply my business major and my past work experience in a way that would satisfy me. Since I liked the creative and performing arts in my personal life and had taken some art courses, I began by looking for an art-business internship. I visited the administrative assistant at the Johnson Art Museum at Cornell to find out more about art administration and what I could expect of the field. Then I used the resource listing books in the Human Ecology Field Study Office and the Career Center to research names of possible internship organizations in the field, located in the Washington area. I came up with a private organization, the Washington Women's Art Center. I wrote using a letter similar to the model letter which follows and received information.

In January, I was planning to visit Washington so I telephoned to arrange interviews. The WWAC planned to "find" things for me to do when nobody was even a full-time worker. I thought about giving up the idea of an internship since it was not going to be what I wanted to do — especially for four months.

Instead, I reevaluated the strategy to find a use for my business major and went back to the resource books to search for internships under the strictly business heading. After reading the available information, I wrote to the business departments of five organizations: two TV stations, the Corporation for Public Broadcasting, a public relations and advertising firm, and the Greater Washington Business Center (a small business-consulting, non-profit organization).

The original description of the desired intern for the GWBC was — "MBA's preferred." "Preferred" isn't "required" so on a chance, I applied anyway. Following any lead, even the smallest, paid off for me. Using the same model letter to ask for information, I eliminated all but the GWBC because their information on the internship work and/or their requirements did not fulfill my expectations and/or requirements. This may have been a mistake on my part. Thinking back, I probably should have tried to interview them anyway. Many organizations, I found out, are willing to negotiate points of the internship and requirements of the prospective intern.

The GWBC sent their information two days before I was intending to visit friends in Washington, so on a chance I telephoned and politely asked for an interview, apologizing for the short notice. The interview was much more extensive and thorough than the others. I toured the three floors of offices, met major officers and was given explanations of all departments and my potential supervisor's duties and responsibilities. Then my supervisor and I sat down to discuss my expectations and what I would like to do with respect to activities and responsibilities.

I learned a tip from my father who sometimes interviews for IBM. He told me that many college graduates and students think that they are superior because they are from a college, deserve instant responsibility and know it all. This attitude is a real turn-off. So I tactfully asked to "help" my supervisor work with clients even though what I wanted was to do his job. Tactfulness and respect, along with tempered honesty went a long way for me. I asked to help him work with clients and much to my surprise and pleasure, he offered to teach me his job and eventually have my own clients. I returned to Cornell, met with Mr. Stanton, Director of the Field Study Office, and wrote the second letter to make permanent arrangements for an internship with the GWBC.

Throughout this process, I think the most productive things I did were: (1) To be persevering, gathering information on one lead and if it didn't work out, go on to another; (2) To be thorough, finding out what the sponsor's requirements were, the requirements of my faculty supervisor and — most especially — my own; (3) To write lots of letters — the more options, the better the chance of finding the right one; and (4) To go to as many interviews as possible. It was only during an interview that I saw my potential workplace, met the supervisor and tested the working atmosphere, asked specific questions regarding my prospective duties and responsibilities. Ultimately this is how I made up my mind about each internship possibility.

One other thing I found important was professionalism in my correspondence, i.e., using correct business form, English and grammar. This, I learned, helped convince my GWBC supervisor that I was *mature enough* and professional enough for the job.

Model Letter for Initial Inquiry

1982 North Campus
Cornell University
Ithaca, New York 14853
February 3, 1982

Mr. Martin S. Drake
Assistant Vice President
Business Development Division
Greater Washington Business Center
1705 DeSales Street, N.W.
Washington, D.C. 20036

Dear Mr. Drake:

Currently I am a student at Cornell University majoring in Business Management and Marketing, and will be receiving my Bachelor of Science degree in December of 1982. For my last semester, I am interested in obtaining an internship in the business field.

After researching possible internship host organizations in my university's Field Study Office, I decided to contact your organization about the possibility of an internship for the Fall of 1982. At this time, I am interested in some more information about your internship program and the Greater Washington Business Center.

Four specific topics of interest to me are: a brief description of your organization's activities, the duties and responsibilities of an intern, the possible arrangements for co-operating with my university's credit requirements, and the application procedure and prerequisites required of a prospective intern. Any other information you would like to provide would also be appreciated.

Thank you for your time and help. I look forward to hearing from you soon.

Sincerely,

Jasmine S. Adham

Jasmine S. Adham

Sample Reply from Internship Organization

GREATER WASHINGTON BUSINESS CENTER
1705 DeSales Street, N.W.
Washington, D.C. 20036

February 13, 1982

Ms. Jasmine S. Adham
1982 North Campus
Cornell University
Ithaca, New York 14853

Dear Ms. Adham

I was pleased to hear from you concerning your interest in the Greater Washington Business Center's (GWBC) internship program. The Center has had great success in working with students from various colleges and universities throughout the states.

GWBC is a private, non-profit business consulting firm under contract with the Minority Business Development Agency (MBDA) of the U.S. Department of Commerce to provide management, financial and technical assistance to small businesses with a specific emphasis on minority firms. Due to budgetary restrictions, the Center is unable to offer an intern any financial assistance other than reimbursement for local travel. Each intern must make his or her own arrangements for securing and maintaining room and board while working with the Center. If internships are eligible for college credits, we will of course cooperate in any feasible manner. Many interns in the past have worked out college credit arrangements with their colleges or universities and were visited by their professors during the internship. All interns are considered regular staff except for remuneration and are expected to perform and dress in a professional manner.

I have enclosed information on the scope of work of GWBC to give you an indication of the type of duties and responsibilities our interns share with regular staff members. I should point out, however, that we allow students maximum responsibility in exercising their assignments. Each intern is assigned a staff supervisor who will orient, monitor and assist the student in the execution of assignments.

If you are still interested in serving an internship with the Center, please forward a copy of your grade transcript and a resume to my attention.

Sincerely yours,

Martin S. Drake,
Assistant Vice President,
Business Development Division

Enclosure

Sample Follow-Up Thank-You Letter

1982 North Campus
Cornell University
Ithaca, N.Y. 14853
March 16, 1982

Mr. Martin S. Drake
Assistant Vice President
Business Development Division
Greater Washington Business Center
1705 DeSales Street, N.W.
Washington, D.C. 20036

Dear Mr. Drake:

I would like to thank you for meeting with me on February 20th especially since it was on such short notice. I returned to Cornell enthusiastic and pleased about the prospect of a Fall internship with the GWBC.

As requested by you, I am enclosing a copy of my current college transcript and resume. I have attached an additional note to my transcript listing my current courses since they are not listed on the official transcript.

Upon my return to Cornell, I met with the director of the Field Study Office, Mr. Timothy Stanton, concerning this prospective internship. Mr. Stanton was pleased with the proposed internship and asked that I contact you concerning three items. First, a letter officially confirming your acceptance of me as an intern for September through December of 1982 is needed by Mr. Stanton in the Field Study Office. Second, three informational brochures detailing the program, the responsibilities of the host organization and the work and responsibilities of the intern are to be sent to you. (I have enclosed these three brochures.) Third, Mr. Stanton will be contacting you sometime within the next few weeks to discuss the proposed internship with you.

Thank you for your time and effort concerning these items. If I can be of any further assistance in completing this process, please contact me. I look forward to serving my internship with the GWBC and with you.

Sincerely,

Jasmine S. Adham
Jasmine S. Adham

Enclosures (5)

Sample of Organization's Acceptance Letter

GREATER WASHINGTON BUSINESS CENTER
1705 DeSales Street, N.W.
Washington, D.C. 20036

March 26, 1982

Ms. Jasmine Adham
1982 North Campus
Cornell University
Ithaca, N.Y. 14853

Re: Internship Program

Dear Ms. Adham:

Please consider this communication as acceptance by the Greater Washington Business Center Internship Program for September through December, 1982.

I am looking forward to speaking with Mr. Stanton and have you work with us.

Sincerely yours,

Martin S. Drake
Assistant Vice President
Business Development Division

MSD/ads

cc: Mr. Timothy Stanton
      Director, Field Study Office
      Cornell University

3

WORKING–LEARNING TIPS

The Working-Learning Equation: Making the Most of Your Internship

"Every worker is a teacher and every workplace is a school because they deal with the real world and man's mastery therein."

Work in America
(a report from the special task force to the Secretary of H.E.W.)

Now that you have an internship, it is time to insure that you make the most of it both as a *working* and as a *learning* experience. As described in the introduction to this handbook, internships are delicate balances between putting out through work and service and taking in through the learning derived from such experiences. If the work or service element seriously outweighs learning in an internship, the experience may become boring and repetitive and lose its educational value. If learning seriously outweighs working or serving, the internship may lose its unique participatory element and resemble a "field trip" rather than an experiential learning experience. The trick is to maintain a fluid balance between the two.

In this chapter we offer a few simple means for monitoring and solving problems in internship work experiences, and some background and techniques for enhancing your ability to learn from the work you will do and the people and environment around you.

What underlies every point made is a complex and sometimes difficult transition you will have to make as an intern. As a student for perhaps thirteen or more years, you have pursued your learning by reading and following signs and directions given to you by teachers and professors. They have been more responsible than you have been for what you have learned. You have been able to see quickly how you were doing through grades on tests, papers and exams. As wonderful or awful as it may have been, it was a generally passive mode of learning. You were only responsible for following directions and assimilating organized material.

As you enter your internship, you will quickly notice a huge change in your relationship to your learning and your success or failure in the internship. Very few people, and possibly no one, will tell you what to learn or how to learn it. The material, knowledge and skills to be acquired will not be well organized or clear and they will be interdependent, intertwined and difficult to sort out. Often you will not know what to do, how to do it, or how you are doing. In other words, a lot of the signs and maps to successful learning, so omnipresent on campus, will be absent; and you are quite likely at times to feel unsure of yourself, rudderless, and reticent about which way to turn. Your friendly professors will not be around to tell you either.

Thus, as you may have desired or expected in your internship, you will be largely on your own and completely responsible for what you learn or fail to learn. You will have to become an active, self-directed worker and learner and you may be surprised at how challenging and difficult that can be.

That is why we have written this chapter — to help you achieve this transition from assimilator to productive worker, from one who is passively led through a set curriculum to one who actively defines what is to be learned and how to learn it.

Working Tips — Tips That Work

Starting Out

It is always important to make a good first impression, so plan carefully how you relate to and interact with your supervisor and co-workers.

Dress. Look for clues from your supervisor and other staff members on dress codes. On the first day, dress neatly, simply and appropriately for your job. If you have questions about your dress, consult with your supervisor.

Promptness. Oversleeping is a poor excuse for being late on the first day or *any* day. Time a test ride to work and plan enough time for breakfast, dressing, etc.

Attitude. Your attitude "is one of your greatest assets." After your appearance, it is the next factor noticed. A positive attitude will benefit you as well as your co-workers.

Agency Rules. Find out about, follow, and respect the regulations of the organization.

Attendance. Arrange in advance when you need to take a day off and try to attend staff meetings and seminars regularly.

Dependability. Whether you work alone or as part of a team, other responsibilities will come your way if your supervisor can depend on you.

Respecting the Time of Others. Consider your supervisor's and staff members' time when seeking help on assignments.

Orientation

Hopefully, your internship supervisor will have prepared the organization for your arrival and have some sort of orientation program for you. The orientation might include:

Reading. Prepare for an avalanche of books and pamphlets that "inform" you. Even if you have done your own homework on the organization, you will probably find new information from your supervisor's personal library.

Meeting Your Co-Workers. Prepare to be whisked around and introduced to lots of people. Try to keep notes as you go so you can later connect names with faces and roles.

Planning Your Internship Activities. Although you should be open and respectful of the plans made by your supervisor, it is never too early to ask questions and state preferences.

Moving In To Your Workspace.   You will need to gather supplies and orient yourself to the physical environment of your internship.

If, for some reason, there is no formal orientation prepared for you, try to give yourself one anyway. Remember, you are now an active learner, responsible for yourself. Just because no one else thinks to orient you does not mean you don't need orientation. Talk to your supervisor about your needs so that you do receive the four items listed above as well as any other information or resources you feel are necessary. In many work environments, staff are overworked and terribly busy. You, as an intern, may fall through the cracks if you don't assert yourself. Generally, internship supervisors not only appreciate your asking or reminding them to do things, but they expect it.

[Note: If you have a *Learning Contract* from your college, orientation is the time to acquaint your supervisor with it if you have not done so already. If you shared your Learning Contract with your supervisor before you arrived at your internship, the orientation period is a good time to review it and make any changes that occur to you or your supervisor now. Even if a contract is not required by your campus, you might consider drawing up an agreement that stipulates the roles and responsibilities of your supervisor. Such a contract will be helpful to refer to later if you and your supervisor have differences over your work assignments. (See Chapter Three for assistance in drawing up a Learning Contract.)]

Getting the Job Done

Once you have been on the job a week or so and begin to know what your assignments are, what your resources are, etc., it is probably time to get organized. Here are few tips to help:*

1. *Schedule Your Time.* Purchase a calendar and schedule your time between free time and committed time (set aside for things you have to do).

2. *Mood Scheduling.* At different times during the day, you are in the mood to tackle different tasks. Plan to work on important chores at the best time of the day for you. If you work better after lunch, start then and use the morning for less important tasks.

3. *Space Out Your Task.* One big task can be broken down into stages.

4. *Reward Yourself.* Plan to give yourself a reward when you finish something important.

5. *Pace Your Energy.* Enthusiasm may overwhelm you at the start and leave you with nothing at the end.

6. *Set Time Limits.* Set time aside to do the things you don't want to do. Put a limit on the time you will spend on that particular task each day until it is finished.

7. *Set Aside Time to Plan.* A time for planning and thinking is needed in your work day. Set aside time to plan and think about your assignments.

8. *Expect the Unexpected.* Give yourself time to finish a project *and* allow for surprises.

Once you are into the swing of work life, organize your schedule and get a feel for what you are doing. Your supervisor may hit you with a large and complicated project. Unlike your professors, he or she probably won't tell you how to do it, just that it needs to be done. The challenge to you is to be an active, independent worker and figure out how to do it. Here are a few tips on planning and problem-solving:

Planning

Begin by organizing the goals or objectives of the project.

1. Decide if some objectives have priority over others for you or your supervisor.
2. Write up your plans for solving the problems or reaching the objectives.
3. Identify the resources you have and the ones you think you need.
4. Consider how and when you expect to gather the resources and complete the project.
5. Share this plan with your supervisor and co-workers to see if they find it realistic. Ask for their suggestions for other ways to go about the job.
6. Refine your plan.

---

* Reproduced by permission from *Glamour* magazine, June 1979, from "Working Smart: How to Get More Done in the Time You Have" by Michael LeBoeuf.

Problem Solving

Regardless of the nature of your projects or work responsibilities, you are bound to run into problems with people, resources or ideas. Most likely you will have to solve them on your own or with little advice from your supervisor or co-workers. Certainly no one will solve these problems for you. If they do, they are robbing you of a valuable learning experience which is why you are on the internship in the first place. In addition, a responsible approach to problem solving is important now because your work affects other people. You are no longer just responsible for yourself and your grades.

There are a number of different methods for solving problems related to work projects. Your supervisor may have some ideas to offer you. Books and journal articles on problem solving line the shelves of libraries. You may want to look for help there. Certainly you have your own individual technique for problem solving which you use every day.

Because of the variety of problems encountered by interns — both work related and interpersonal and the variety of interns and their approaches to problem solving, we hesitate to give specific do's and don'ts in this area, but we like the diagram developed by Dr. Frank Betts and Roberta DeHaan of the Great Lakes Colleges Association Philadelphia Urban Semester Program. It is an organized way of thinking through the solution to a problem and a plan for action. It reminds you to be careful to judge when a problem is yours and when it is someone else's. Take a look at Betts' model in relation to a problem you are facing right now and see if you find it useful.

Problem Solving Model

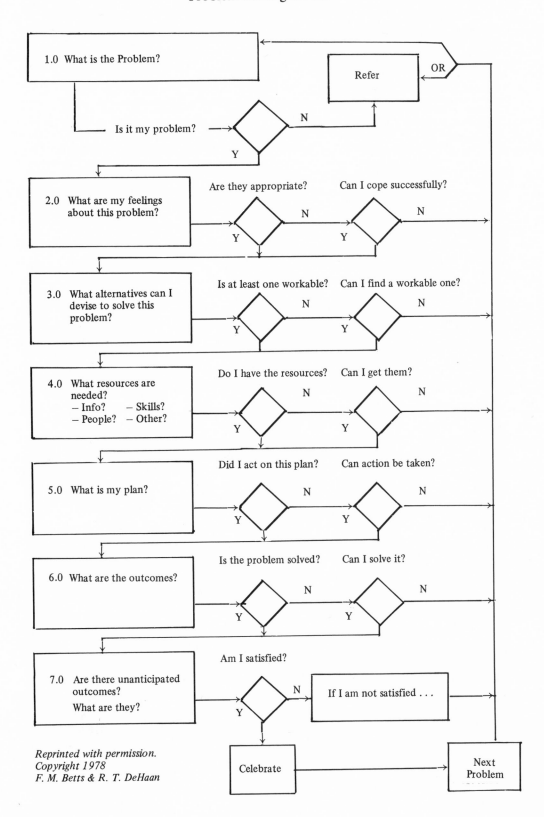

Expecting problems also helps prepare you for them. Deal with them; don't ignore them. You are capable of making the decision between something you can handle and something to take to your supervisor. Here are a few typical problem situations with potential solutions:

Problems with Work Assignments

"Go fer" Work. Everyone in a work setting may eventually be asked to "go fer" work. The routine jobs play an important role in the effective operation of any organization. As a member of a "team" you will want to chip in when necessary even if, for example, stuffing envelopes was not a part of the job description. However, you may not want it to become your permanent job. Consult your supervisor if you feel your work activities are not challenging you intellectually, emotionally and in certain skill and experience areas. Use your objectives outlined in Chapter Two, Step One, and your Learning Contract or work agreement made with your supervisor as a way to remind him or her why you are there.

Additional Responsibilities. At the same time, be sensitive about requesting additional tasks and responsibilities. The success of assigned tasks is evidence of your ability and willingness to complete delegated work. Before you ask for extra assignments, be sure that you can handle them and that you have demonstrated your capacity to handle them. Remember as well that part of maintaining the delicate balance between working and learning is being aware of the balance that must exist between your needs as. a learner and your organization's need to serve clients or customers. Be aware that you will not always get what you want. Be aware of the richness of that sort of experience and how you can learn to cope and grow from failure as well as from success.

Personal Time. As an intern, your first priority and commitment must be to your supervisor and the organization. If you have extra work to do for your faculty supervisor back on campus, you may have to do it on your own time. Seminars, tours, discussion sessions, etc., are educational activities you should attend, but there must be a balance between attending these activities and fulfilling your other duties.

Pressure. Meeting deadlines is your responsibility, but if the pressure to finish assignments on time begins to overwhelm you, let your supervisor know. The quality of your work is as important as the time element. The best planning can fall through, so don't be afraid to say you can't finish on time or you think that the project is too much for you to handle.

One of the greatest pitfalls of interns is a tendency to assume that supervisors know everything an intern is doing and how he or she feels about it. There is a propensity to see supervisors as all-seeing and superhuman. Actually, of course, they are more like you than not. And, like you, they need to be told how you are doing and how you feel about it because they may be too busy or forget to ask. Don't be afraid to speak up. It's your responsibility as an independent learner and worker and no one else will do it for you. Having unrealistic expectations of your supervisor is as unfair to him or her as it is to you.

Problems with Co-Workers

Resentment. Some interns discover, much to their surprise, that co-workers resent them because of the special nature and flexibility built into most internships. After all, your co-workers are not allowed to interview the vice president or attend board meetings, as you might be able to do. It is your supervisor's responsibility to explain your role to fellow employees, but you can help by being sensitive to this issue and sticking to the role of "regular" employee as much as possible. Also, be curious. Co-workers may enjoy having interns around as new folks to talk to and as people with new, fresh perspectives on the workplace. Conversation and open exchange is your best route to good relationships with other members of the staff. Avoid petty internal struggles and do not yield to pressure to take sides when it is inappropriate, which it usually will be.

Overtime. The working world doesn't stop every day at 5:00 PM and you may be asked or simply feel pressure to work late or on weekends. This is another tricky issue which you have to resolve yourself. Working extra hours may help you learn more from your internship by experiencing roles or situations not otherwise available. Your commitment to your supervisor, your project, and/or the organization may demand that you put in the extra work. However, on the other side, you are an independent person just like any other employee and have to make a judgment about when enough is enough. Everyone has a personal life and relationship to maintain. As an intern in a new city, part of your learning, understandably, should come from living in and exploring this new environment. So, if you find yourself confused about work hours and time, talk to your supervisor and negotiate a solution that takes into account your needs and those of the organization. This is a crucial work skill and you might as well start learning it right now.

Communication. You are a member of a project team and you begin to feel as though your ideas don't count, aren't good enough or are ignored. This may be true and thus require action. On the other hand, you may not be letting people know what you have to offer. Before you get upset, examine your participation and be sure that you have really communicated your thoughts. If you are having trouble doing this, find an "ally" in the office and ask for help!

Discrimination. If you feel you are truly being discriminated against because of age, sex or race, you will also have to check this out with the people involved. Don't over-react. Remember, it is possible that people feel threatened by you just as you feel threatened by them. So consider the situation from all angles before you consult your supervisor. But don't let these problems fester. If you have decided the problem is real, deal with it quickly. You are only there for a semester or a summer and time's a-wasting.

Sexual Harassment. You are being sexually harassed on the job. Use tact in deal-with an "overly friendly" boss or co-worker. You should inform the person immediately and politely about behavior you find offensive. Optimistically, the situation could resolve itself. Realistically, it will remain a problem unless you take action to resolve it. Ask for help from co-workers if you feel you need it.

Most of you will not run into these particular problems but a few of you may and you should not be surprised if you do. They are typical "real world" problems, and learning to deal with them is why you are on the internship.

A positive frame of mind is your best support. You are not an expert but you are a capable individual. Remember that. Be sure of *yourself* and stay that way. Setbacks and disappointments will come but, by remembering who you are, you will be in a better position to handle them when they arise. Keep them in perspective and don't consider them to be a personal condemnation of your abilities because they are not necessarily related to you or your actions at all. They are simply there and part of the game.

Here is an example of how one student, an intern in a state assembly-woman's office, handled some of these problems. She describes what she did in a journal she kept for her faculty sponsor.

JANE DAY'S JOURNAL

I am accustomed to depending on external forces (professors) to initiate and direct my learning. I had been dissatisfied with my placement in Sarah Wilson White's office. My work had been too mechanical. I worked on the calendar of bills and committee agendas but this didn't involve much intellectual effort. I spoke with Sarah at a staff meeting and she assured me that this was temporary and that I would soon be given meaningful work. My uneasiness was assuaged but as time passed and the situation did not change, I became increasingly frustrated. I went to my supervisor, Janet Ward, and explained my feelings about the situation. She told me it was "temporary" again, but I pointed out the considerable amount of time that had passed since my talk with Sarah. Janet then told Sarah that I felt I was over my head in work. This comment had nothing to do with my situation. Obviously we had not communicated. I stepped in and tried to explain what I had meant. Sarah, however, was in a bad mood that day and did not want to hear any complaints. She brushed me off with a "we'll talk about it later" and that was the end of that. Janet gave me a substantive assignment that day but hasn't since. From this situation and another, I concluded that my learning objectives could only be fulfilled as a result of my own initiative.

As a result of the situation in the office, I decided to get involved in an outside research project. I went to Alice Richards, the chairperson of the Program and Committee Staff for Child Care. She came up with the idea for a demonstration bill and gave it to another intern and me to research. The idea has developed into a major issue. It is going to be a program bill which will help in its passage. A member of Speaker Knight's staff is very enthusiastic about it and the speaker may sponsor the bill.

However, when my work for the senior citizen/child day care center was finished, the mechanical nature of my office assignments became more apparent than ever. I was becoming increasingly disturbed by the fact that the majority of my time was being spent on essentially clerical duties. Knowledge of the backgrounds of and interactions between my fellow workers did not help me secure more substantive work. I felt as if I was up against a brick wall. Each staff member wanted as much legislative responsibility as possible and there didn't seem to be anything I could do to obtain any of it. I was resigned to having to go outside the office to get meaningful work. My discussion with Lela Park, director of the Intern Program, confirmed my resignation. She gave me support by telling me that former interns with similar office situations had made their internships worthwhile by going outside the office to the research staff and agencies.

Next I had my small group discussion meeting. Groups of ten to fifteen interns meet with the professor-in-residence two times per semester to talk about their placements, what they are doing and how they feel about it. One intern said she was not being given any substantive work either. Determined to become an essential staff member, she refused to go outside the office to obtain meaningful work. Her persistence angered a co-worker so that they weren't on speaking terms. The intern decided the Assemblyman was her only hope, but he had no time to sit and talk with her. She figured the only place to get his attention was in the car driving down to the district where interruptions were impossible. She then took an unannounced trip to the district with the Assemblyman. They spoke for hours and he was very impressed with her intelligence and experience, both of which he had previously been too busy to discover. From then on, she has been an integral and accepted member of the office, receiving substantive assignments from the legislator and the staff.

This small group discussion spurred me to take further action in my office. I finally admitted to myself that I had been scared of antagonizing my co-workers. I felt I wouldn't be able to work in a situation where people resented me. This intern's example showed me that it's not a crime to be aggressive, that I have a right to fight for what I want. Yes, it's necessary to do my share of the mechanical work but as an intern my primary task is to learn. The small group discussion also showed me that if I anger a staff member, the situation is not irrevocable and the other intern and her co-worker are now on speaking terms.

I then began keeping a journal of how I spent each day. I recorded the number of hours spent on each task. After deciding to approach the staff one last time before I went to Sarah, I showed Janet the journal and told her how ridiculous it was to waste such a valuable resource. She agreed and told me she had not realized I had been spending so much time on mechanical work. I felt I had made this quite clear, but it was not necessary to argue the point. She said she'd work something out and let me know the following day. The next morning, Sarah told me I would be working with Rita Connor, counsel for the Legislative Task Force on Women's Issues.

I am quite satisfied with the work I am doing for Rita. I have worked on the package of rape legislation and I am now researching incest. I even spoke at a women's study group on child sexual abuse and showed a film on incest. I am learning a great deal and Sarah likes my work so much that she has asked me to do research for the Legislative Task Force on Women's Issues this summer.

The following is another example of how a student working in a consumer affairs program dealt with a problem she encountered in her internship. She describes it in her journal.

MARY SMITH'S JOURNAL

I cannot say that I was not forewarned by my placement sponsor as to the long hours involved in public interest work. However, it was not until this particular incident that I began to understand the true length of time that he was referring to.

On my second day of work, I was surprised to hear that the staff was invited and encouraged to attend a television taping session featuring our boss. The event was to take place between three-thirty and five-thirty that afternoon at Georgetown University, located across the town from our office. It was my belief that I would have a shortened work day due to this activity and I was quite pleased after having arrived at work somewhat early that morning.

I suppose that I should have gotten the hint when we left no sooner than three-fifteen to get there, but I naively assumed that everyone was simply running a little behind schedule. We got there on time, regardless of our departure time, and were treated to a terrifically exciting performance. I really felt a part of our enthusiastic group and figured that we would all go out and celebrate the huge success of the show. Apparently the staff had a different idea. When we got on the bus, I realized that our destination was not "party" oriented. My stomach tightened as we passed the stop near my house on the way back to the office. The office? That is correct. Everyone was going back to work at six-fifteen.

As soon as we got in the office, John Rochester, my "tell it like it is" supervisor, assigned me another two hours worth of work. At first I thought that he was kidding, so I laughed right to his face when he handed me the assignments. He just asked me what was so humorous. I was so embarrassed, confused, angry, annoyed and tired. I was very disappointed with myself for not having taken his "long hours" warning seriously.

This incident had quite an effect on me. To begin with, it definitely exposed me to the role and activities of a consumer activist. Apparently, "all nighters" do not end with college in public interest work. The staff, as consequent days have verified, is expected to work on an extremely grueling schedule. I believe that I was able to gain insight as to what it takes to make the grade in this office. I cannot say that it is a pleasing realization, but an important and necessary one for me.

This incident has also taught me to accept and deal with the long, intense hours of work. I do not find myself anticipating a six o'clock dinner anymore. I have changed my working, sleeping and eating schedule to cope with the time demands. In order to be able to truly integrate with this world, I have no choice but to adjust my life style. I cannot say that I want this to be my permanent way of living. However, for me to obtain the true perspective of public interest work, I believe such self-alterations are necessary during this internship.

Your Progress

At various stages of your internship, you should quiz yourself on your own progress. Compare the changes in your attitude as well as changes in your projects and assignments. Questions to ask:

1. Are you meeting deadlines?

2. Are you using work time efficiently?

3. How are you using your personal skills/knowledge?

4. Are you using information you learned in courses at school?

5. How well are you performing under supervision? Without supervision?

6. Evaluate your approach methods for each assignment.

7. Are you enjoying it? Effective working and learning is fun. If your internship is a drag, figure out why and do something about it.

Concluding the Internship

So much effort goes into preparing for internships and succeeding at them that we sometimes lose sight of the fact that they are transitory, short-term experiences with problems peculiar to their unique time span.

Some closing tips:

1. If your internship requires you to work with clients or customers, be sure they know in advance *when you are leaving* and *why you are leaving*. The fact that you don't show up one Monday morning can be damaging to an organization's service — particularly if you are working with people who came to depend on you for certain tangible or intangible resources. This is particularly important if you are working with children or others who don't have the slightest notion of what an internship is or why you are on one.

2. Bring closure to your other working relationships. Relationships need care and maintenance whether they are ending with the internship or continuing.

3. Organize your work projects in such a way that someone else can continue them. You won't win many points from your supervisor if you leave your work in a tangled mass out of which he or she or someone else has to make sense and continue.

4. Be sure to communicate the appreciation you feel to co-workers, supervisors and others for the attention and care they gave you while you were on the internship. They didn't *have* to do it.

LEARNING TIPS

Field experience learning may be a new wrinkle on an old time-worn practice, but because it is familiar doesn't mean it's easy. In fact, learning how to learn from fluid, dynamic experiences in which you have a part may actually be more difficult than anything you have every tried. Why? Think about it for a minute. Remember your last summer job and see if you can articulate to yourself what you learned. When did you know you had learned it? What factors, incidents, actions helped you learn it or hindered your learning it? Probably it is very hard for you to say. Most likely you can identify most easily what you learned. Exactly how you learned it is more difficult to pinpoint.

The information that follows is presented on the premise that we do not simply "learn from experience" or by accident. We feel that there are techniques and activities which can not only enhance your learning while you are on your internship, but also help you articulate what you learn and conceptualize how you learned it.

Besides helping to insure the learning part of the internship equation, this section of the manual will also be useful to those of you who need to document the reflection and thinking you do in your internship in order to earn academic credit. Think about the ideas and structures that follow as you plan your learning contract or agreement with your faculty supervisor. Refer to them regularly while you are on the job. Knowing concretely what you "studied" and what you learned on your internship will help you justify earning those credits when you get back to campus. Perhaps more importantly, knowing what you got out of your internship will help you figure out what working or learning step is best for you following your internship.

What Is Experiential Learning? Some Background

A simple way of looking at field experience learning was derived by Dr. David Kolb at Case Western Reserve University's School of Public Management.* It looks like this:

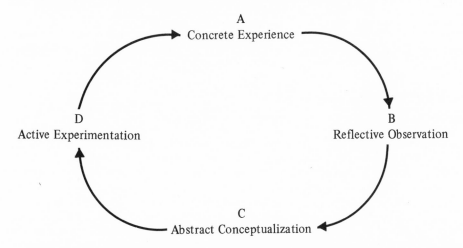

As an experiential learner on an internship, you engage in (A) concrete experience (your work assignment — the doing part of your internship). At night, on coffee breaks, on the subway, or even while you work you (B) reflect on this experience, perhaps "meditate" is a better word. And out of this reflection or rumination, you consciously or unconsciously form (C) theories, concepts and ideas about your experience.

For example, you have been doing a lot of (A) legislative research on your internship. In reflecting on the experience, you (B) begin to wonder how policies really become laws and sense that you are really happy while doing the research. Out of this reflection, some ideas (C) pop into your mind. Who speaks for the consumer when regulations for the Federal Trade Commission are enacted? Maybe I would like a career or post-graduate study that involves this kind of work.

What follows this theory, or idea-forming, stage according to Kolb is active experimentation. You take your ideas about consumer participation in the creation of FTC regulations and ask your supervisor and co-workers about them. When doing your research, you look for more answers or clues that will support or change your ideas about who is represented in the creation of legislation. On the personal side, you monitor yourself to see what aspects of this research really turn you on, and you ask your supervisor and co-workers how they got involved in this work, what they like about it and what sort of preparation you would need to pursue it as a career.

In applying (D) your ideas to your experience in this way, your experience (A) changes and generates new reflections (B) and new theories or ideas (C) in you, and you apply them (D) to the experience (A) again, changing it and you once again, and so on. Such is Kolb's learning cycle.

---

* From *Learning Style Inventory Technical Manual* by David A. Kolb. Boston, Mass., McBer and Company, 1976.

Now, obviously, you don't go through such an organized, structured thinking process as you experience each facet of your internship. However, Kolb suggests that your thinking passes through these stages to some degree all the time in regard to all of your experience and he goes on to demonstrate that all of us have different strengths in different stages of the process. Some of us are good at reflecting on our experiences; others of us prefer and are better at applying our theories to experience and tinkering with them, while others of us may excel at and prefer deriving theories from our reflections and avoid actual experience as much as possible. Which is your pattern?

Regardless of your response, three points about experiential learning as described this way are important.

1.   *You must be active in the learning process.* As we have stated earlier, experiential learning is active learning and you will need to push yourself through the learning stages with which you are less comfortable. For instance, as one in love with and effective at getting involved in and experiencing life, you may enjoy the activity of your internship, but you may have to discipline yourself to sit back and reflect on what you are doing in order to insure that you really learn from it, that you know what you are learning, and that what you learn includes what you want to learn. If you are the reflective type of person with a tendency to let others do the active work, in order to get the most out of your internship you may have to put energy into forcing yourself to take more initiative to ask questions and take on varied and challenging work assignments that otherwise might pass you by.

2.   *You, the learner, are the one who determines what you want to learn.* Internships enable you to create your own curriculum and you will need to give your experience focus in order not to be overwhelmed by the amount and variety of potential data and phenomena to absorb. In this active mode of learning, you are the professor of the course. Your experience, your supervisor, your faculty sponsor, co-workers, other interns, etc., are learning resources to be tapped thoughtfully and carefully.

3.   *You are more conscious of what you are learning and how to learn it.* If you are engaged in an active learning process with responsibility for what and how you learn, you will need to monitor continually and evaluate the progress you make toward achieving your learning and accomplishing goals for your internship while you are on the job.

None of this should come as news to you. As you read along, you probably find yourself saying to yourself — yes, I do that. Yes, I think about and analyze my experiences all the time. We all do. What follows, however, are some useful structures and techniques for making your experiential learning process while on an internship more active, more conscious and more productive.

Start with Objectives

As in any dynamic experience, internships introduce you to so much new activity, new environments, new people, new knowledge, etc., that they can quickly become overwhelming. Experiencing and dealing with this multifaceted and serendipitous nature of internships is one of their chief assets and attractions as well as one of their major challenges. Whether you use a learning contract or not, setting and monitoring learning objectives is a useful means for planning and evaluating your active learning and sorting out what aspects of an internship are *most important to you* to learn and understand, and which aspects you may want to pay less attention to. Objectives are a rational way for you to decide consciously what you want to learn and avoid being "blown out" by all the new input and experiences you encounter.

Here are some steps to developing sound learning objectives:

1. Again, we ask you to go back to Step One in Chapter Two and look at the notes you wrote as to why you wanted an internship in the first place. Examine those objectives *after you have been on the job for a couple of weeks,* and see if they still make sense. Then refine and rewrite them. The techniques for developing objectives in Step One will be useful again now.

2. Once you have come up with some statements that make sense to you, share them with your internship supervisor. Does he/she think they are realistic based on his/her knowledge of what you will be doing and observing? Talk with your supervisor about which of your activities will lend themselves more or less to which objectives and then refine and rewrite them again.

3. If you have not done so already, share your objectives with your academic faculty sponsor on campus. After all, as a self-directed learner, you want your school to know what you wish to be held accountable for and what you are not interested in.

4. See if you can conceive of some means for knowing whether, or to what extent, you have reached these learning objectives at the conclusion of your internship. How will you know whether you have learned what you set out to learn? How might you evaluate your internship in relation to your objectives?

5. Put these objectives away until the mid-point of your internship. Then pull them out and examine them to see how you are doing. Are you making progress toward them? Are they still what you want to learn? Do you have additions or deletions? If you are not making progress, do you need to change your internship activities? Do you need to change your objectives? Communicate with your internship supervisor and, if possible, your academic sponsor about your conclusions. Rewrite your objectives again, if they need revision. Improve your internship if it needs it.

6. Keep your new and old objectives for evaluation purposes at the end of your internship. (See Chapter Four.)

The Learning Contract

Learning contracts are outlines of what you intend to learn and accomplish while you are on your internship. They are effective tools for gaining agreement between you, your internship supervisor and your faculty sponsor on your mutual intentions and expectations for the internship, both educational and work-related as well as on criteria and techniques for grading and evaluation at the internship's conclusion.

Many internship programs require interns and internship supervisors to complete learning contracts before the internship begins in order to be certain that both parties understand and agree to the role and work responsibilities to be carried out by the student and the supervision to be provided by the supervisor. Many college field experience education directors (or faculty who sponsor student interns) utilize learning contracts to develop work and supervision agreements which outline the commitments made by the student and faculty members, thus spelling out the rationale for granting academic credit for the internship.

Since grading of experiential learning is such a complicated and thorny issue, learning contracts are often used to clarify student's learning objectives and determine agreed-upon bases for grading. In all cases, such agreements — no matter who has initiated them — help all three parties in an internship (students, faculty, internship supervisors) develop clear understandings of what they expect of each other at the outset of an internship, understandings they can refer to later if differences or problems arise.

There is a tremendous variety of learning contract forms and designs. If you have a faculty sponsor or are participating in an internship program that requires completing a learning contract, you will probably use their forms. What follows is a learning contract form for use by students who are not required to write such agreements but who wish to obtain agreements on intentions and expectations from their faculty sponsor and internship supervisor before they leave campus or, at least, by the first or second week of the internship.

A sample learning contract appears on the following pages, filled in to give you an idea of what to include in your own contract. Then a blank contract is provided for your own use.

Part I is for the "nuts and bolts" of your internship and should be easy to fill out.

Parts II and III require more thought on your part. Begin by drafting and refining your ideas on blank sheets of paper. Read pertinent sections of this manual for assistance. (For example, to write learning objectives, refer back to the preceding page; for evaluation ideas, see Chapter Four.) Allow time to show your draft to your faculty sponsor and internship supervisor (by mail, if necessary) for their reactions and revisions. When you have something you feel good about and everyone agrees to, write it into your contract.

Go slowly with this stage, whether you do it on campus before you start your internship or during the first week or two on the job. Thinking through your learning and accomplishing objectives and carefully stating them to yourself and your sponsor and supervisor will help you focus your energies for the internship. As an active, experiential learner, this is your first opportunity to design your own curriculum. Writing up your internship work assignments and stating your expectations for supervision enables you to gain or negotiate a clear understanding of what will happen when you arrive at your workplace. Be thoughtful about it and give yourself enough time — weeks, if you need to use the mails.

Part IV, the signatures signifying agreement, should be simple if you have involved your faculty sponsor and internship supervisor in the preparation of the contract. If you have not involved them, you are likely to have your contract rejected by one or both of them. *Do it right the first time.*

Once you have an agreed-upon contract, you have something to rely on if problems crop up on your internship. If you feel you are not getting the expected supervision on the job, call your supervisor's attention to the contract. If you feel your faculty sponsor is demanding too much or different work than you expected, remind him or her of the contract. If you find yourself changing your objectives or intentions for the internship, take a look at the contract and see if you can figure out why. If you are serious about these changes, amend your contract and seek agreement again from your advisor and supervisor.

Using a learning contract in this way is a good technique for keeping in touch with yourself, your faculty sponsor and internship supervisor during an internship and communicating clearly about its most important element — your experience. Try it!

Sample Learning Contract

LEARNING CONTRACT

PART I:

A. Name: JAMES MONROE   Social Security No.: 012-34-5678

    Campus Address: Home Address:

    901 Morgan Tower   100 Main Street
            (street)   (street)
    S.U.N.Y., Syracuse, New York 13210   Palmyra, New York 14522
    (city)   (state)   (zip)   (city)   (state)   (zip)
    (315) 456-2121   (315) 555-1212
        (telephone)   (telephone)

    Address while on internship:

            222 E. Pleasant St., Apt. 4
                (street)
            Albany, New York 12207
            (city)   (state)   (zip)
            (518) 211-1234
                (telephone)

B. Internship Organization: Office of Assemblyman, Henry Dinardo, State Assembly

    Address: New York State Capitol

    Telephone: (518) 678-1000, Ext. 345

    Name of Supervisor: Ingrid Martin   Position: Senior Political Advisor

    Your Position: Legislative Aide

C. Faculty Sponsor/Advisor: Lela Copeland

    Department: Government

    Address: State University of New York, Syracuse, NY 13210

    Telephone: (315) 324-7200

D. Credits to be awarded for internship: Government   402   15
                             Department   Course No. No. of Credits

Sample Learning Contract — Continued

PART II: THE INTERNSHIP

A. JOB DESCRIPTION: Describe in as much detail as possible your role and responsibilities while on your internship. List duties, projects to be completed, deadlines, etc., if relevant.

Acting as legislative aid, I understand that I will be responsible for doing background research on legislative issues under consideration in the State Assembly. This research will involve library work, telephone inquiries, and field visits to constituent agencies and organizations. I will be required to write background papers on my findings by deadlines to be determined by my supervisor. I will provide general assistance in the office -- to be determined by my supervisor. I will provide clerical assistance in the office -- telephone answering, reception, messenger service -- on an occasional basis, as needed. I will work 40 hours per week and overtime as needed.

B. SUPERVISION: Describe in as much detail as possible the supervision to be provided. What kind of instruction, assistance, consultation, etc., you will receive from whom, etc.

I will meet weekly with my supervisor to monitor the progress of my research and learn about implications and results of my findings, and the status of relevant legislation. I will receive instruction on the use of the State Library from other research staff in the office. I will visit the district office once every two or three weeks for consultation with its staff and constituents on issues under my attention. Bradley Smith, Office Manager, will give me a general orientation and assist me as needed in performing general office tasks.

C. EVALUATION: How will your work performance be evaluated? By whom? When?

My work will be evaluated by my supervisor and myself in a final consultation session. We will use a standard state employee evaluation form as well.

PART III: LEARNING OBJECTIVES/LEARNING ACTIVITIES/EVALUATION

A. LEARNING OBJECTIVES: What do you intend to learn through this experience? Be specific. Try to use concrete, measurable terms.

(1) I will be able to describe how public policy is developed and enacted in the state legislature.

(2) I will understand the role and activities of an Assemblyman.

(3) I will examine and develop an in-depth understanding of the involvement of racial minorities in the development of at least two major pieces of social policy legislation in the state and the consequences for these people as a result of its enactment or lack of enactment in the legislature.

(4) I will develop and practice legislative research and report writing.

(5) I will improve communication skills -- writing, conversing, etc.

Sample Learning Contract — Continued

B.   LEARNING ACTIVITIES:

(1)   **On-the-Job:** Describe how your internship activities will enable you to meet your learning objectives. Include projects, research, report writing, conversations, etc., which you will do while working, relating them to what you intend to learn.

By working in Assemblyman Dinardo's office, consulting with my supervisor and co-workers, by following legislation from initiation to enactment, by researching its need and impact, by visiting constituents, by writing reports, by having to communicate clearly by telephone, memo, etc., I will be able to attain my learning objectives.

(2)   **Off-the-Job:** List reading, writing, contact with faculty sponsor, peer group, discussion, field trips, observations, etc., you will make and carry out which will help you meet your learning objectives.

During my internship, I will read two books on public policy to be assigned by my faculty sponsor. I will keep a journal of my activities. I will submit three evaluative reports to my sponsor on my progress in my internship. I will talk to other student interns and I will participate in political-social functions.

At the conclusion of my internship, I will write two papers. One will be a self-evaluation of my progress made toward meeting learning objectives. The other will be a term paper (10-15 pages) following the legislative history of a major social policy issue in this year's legislative session and focusing on the involvement of Hispanic Americans in its development and enactment and its probable impact on their lives.

C.   EVALUATION: How will you know what you have learned, or that you have achieved your learning objectives? How do you wish to evaluate your progress toward meeting these objectives? Who will evaluate? When? How will a grade be determined? By whom? When?

Evaluation of my progress made toward my learning objectives through this internship will be done in the following ways: Objectives 1, 2, 3 and 5 through my term paper, my self-evaluation report and through conversations with my faculty sponsor. Objective 4 by feedback from my internship supervisor and faculty advisor on reports that I write on my legislative research.

My grade will be determined by my faculty sponsor who will take into account my self-evaluation and evaluation of my internship supervisor of my work performance.

PART IV: AGREEMENT

This contract may be terminated or amended by student, faculty sponsor or internship supervisor at any time upon written notice, which is received and agreed to by the other two parties.

Student Signature:_____ Date:_____

Faculty Sponsor: _____ Date:_____

Internship Supervisor:_____ Date:_____

(Copies of this contract should be distributed to all parties.)

SAMPLE LEARNING CONTRACT

LEARNING CONTRACT

PART I:

A. Name: _____   Social Security No.:_____

Campus Address: Home Address:

_____   _____
      (street)   (street)

_____   _____
(city)   (state)   (zip)   (city)   (state)   (zip)

_____   _____
    (telephone)   (telephone)

Address while on internship:

_____
      (street)

_____
(city)   (state)   (zip)

_____
     (telephone)

B. Internship Organization: _____

   Address: _____

   Telephone: _____

   Name of Supervisor: _____   Position: _____

   Your Position: _____

C. Faculty Sponsor/Advisor: _____

   Department: _____

   Address: _____

   Telephone: _____

D. Credits to be awarded for internship: _____ _____ _____
                                      Department   Course No. No. of Credits

Sample Learning Contract — Continued

PART II: THE INTERNSHIP

A.   JOB DESCRIPTION: Describe in as much detail as possible your role and responsibilities while on your internship. List duties, projects to be completed, deadlines, etc., if relevant.

B.   SUPERVISION: Describe in as much detail as possible the supervision to be provided. What kind of instruction, assistance, consultation, etc., you will receive from whom, etc.

C.   EVALUATION: How will your work performance be evaluated? By whom? When?

PART III: LEARNING OBJECTIVES/LEARNING ACTIVITIES/EVALUATION

A.   LEARNING OBJECTIVES: What do you intend to learn through this experience? Be specific. Try to use concrete, measurable terms.

Sample Learning Contract — Continued

B. **LEARNING ACTIVITIES:**

  (1) **On-the-Job:** Describe how your internship activities will enable you to meet your learning objectives. Include projects, research, report writing, conversations, etc., which you will do while working, relating them to what you intend to learn.

  (2) **Off-the-Job:** List reading, writing, contact with faculty sponsor, peer group, discussion, field trips, observations, etc., you will make and carry out which will help you meet your learning objectives.

C. **EVALUATION:** How will you know what you have learned, or that you have achieved your learning objectives? How do you wish to evaluate your progress toward meeting these objectives? Who will evaluate? When? How will a grade be determined? By whom? When?

PART IV: AGREEMENT

This contract may be terminated or amended by student, faculty sponsor or internship supervisor at any time upon written notice, which is received and agreed to by the other two parties.

Student Signature:_____ Date:_____

Faculty Sponsor: _____ Date:_____

Internship Supervisor:_____ Date:_____

(Copies of this contract should be distributed to all parties.)

Monitor Yourself, Your Learning and Your Internship Experience

Keeping a Journal

There are a variety of ways to write and keep journals. You may already be doing one on your own. Your internship supervisor or faculty sponsor may require you to keep one. In either case, journals are an excellent way to improve and document your active, conscious reflections on your internship experience.

We offer the following technique as a particularly useful one for field learners. It is not terribly time-consuming. It can be both intensive and enjoyable to write, and it ties directly into your work on objectives.

Reflection and Conceptualization: The Critical Incident Technique

A field journal is a collection of notes on your observations, reflective thoughts, questions and feelings about your off-campus learning experience. If you keep a journal, like an anthropologist in the field, you may choose to take notes on the activities around you, the people you work with, and the general atmosphere surrounding your work. You would probably describe events as they occur, with no predetermined emphasis, usually in ordinary time sequence. You would sort out items to record from the myriad of events in your day, consciously, or more probably unconsciously according to your own values, interests or even whims. And, in spite of the value of such a recording and thinking process, essential elements of your field experience, because they did not happen to interest you that day or because they just did not *seem* important to you at the time, would often get lost or ignored.

What follows is a much more structured but, we believe, more useful journal-keeping technique which helps you monitor and evaluate your internship experience in relation to the specific goals and learning objectives you set for your experience.

The Critical Incident Journal Technique*

The "critical incident" journal technique differs in many ways from the more informal journal writing described above. *First, the writer uses preset objectives as criteria for determining what incidents from his/her field experience to select for recording and analysis.* These objectives may be stipulated by a fieldwork course instructor or mentor, or they may be individually conceived and determined by the writer based on his or her personal objectives for undertaking an internship.

---

* Information for this section was drawn from the following sources:

John Flanagan, "The Critical Incident Technique" in *Psychological Bulletin.* July 1954, Vol. 51, No. 4, pp. 327-358.

John Duley, "Cross-Cultural Field Study" in *Implementing Field Experience Education, New Directions for Higher Education, No. 6,* Summer 1974, pp. 13-22.

Gilbert Robinson, "About Your Journal," unpublished memo to Students of Center for Institutional Change, San Francisco State University, San Francisco, California 94132.

Timothy Stanton, "Skills Building Assignment No. 5 Reflection and Conceptualization: The Critical Incident Technique," Field Study Office, New York State College of Human Ecology, Cornell University, Ithaca, New York 14853.

Second in a "critical incident" journal *the writer chooses incidents from his or her field experience according to the change they produce in him or her.* Rather than a record of daily life in the field, a "critical incident" journal should include detailed accounts of *only those incidents which change you or your perspective in terms of your learning objectives,* your assumed role as an intern or the general impact they have on you as a person.

Third, "critical incident" journals contain reflection on incidents that are not necessarily treated in normal time sequence. Chronological time is not an important criteria for deciding what incidents to include in a journal and how to include them. Their impact on you, even if you do not become aware of that impact until you experience several other incidents, is far more important.

The *fourth,* and perhaps most important element in "critical incident" journal keeping *is that the writer uses the recording and analysis of selected incidents to measure his/her individual progress toward reaching his/her identified learning objectives and progress as an intern.* Rather than simply describing and interpreting an incident and the people involved, this reflection and conceptualization technique enables the writer to use the incident and its impact as a means for self-monitoring and personal exploration.

Obviously, in keeping this sort of a record, no two people will consider the same two incidents as critical. For example, an intern working in a youth agency may alter his/her perception of himself or herself of human development, or, of his/her field placement as a result of an altercation with a particular youth and thus wish to explore this incident in his/her journal. Yet, to another intern, the same confrontation could be a minor incident having little personal or educational impact and, therefore, not merit inclusion.

Whether to include an incident or not depends on how it relates to why you have chosen to be an intern and what you are trying to get out of the experience. Consider yourself a pool ball in progress across the table. In a "critical incident" journal, you will want to record and explore the points of impact with other balls which cause you to change your direction. You will want to describe and explore in writing both the incident of impact and how it affected your progress as an intern. At first, it will be difficult to determine which incidents comprise these "points of impact." However, as time goes on you will become increasingly adept at recognizing a pattern in the kind of incidents which have a powerful effect on you. This understanding of your own patterns, alone, should prove extremely useful to you in making key decisions later on.

We recommend that you sit down at least once a week and choose one or two critical (to you) incidents that have taken place during the week and explore them in detail in your journal. Remember, "critical" means having strong impact on you in terms of your objectives. Here are some steps for organizing your reflecting and writing.

(1) *Identify* the event or occurrence with as much specificity as possible — the problem to be solved, issues involved, etc.

(2) *Describe* the relevant details and circumstances surrounding the event so that you and any possible readers will understand what happened. What? When? How? Why? Where?

(3) *List* the people involved, describe them and their relationship to you and to each other. (Who?)

(4) *Describe your role* in the situation — what you did, how you acted.

(5) *Analyze* the incident. How well or badly did you understand the situation? How did you handle it? What would you do differently the next time? Why?

(6) *Analyze this incident in terms of its impact on you* and explain why you view it as "critical." How does it relate to your particular learning objective(s)? What have you learned from the experience? How has your perspective on yourself been changed and/or reinforced? Where do you go from here?

In spite of the complexity of this sort of writing, your journal entries need not be long nor arduous. The importance of this exercise is learning *to sift through your experience for what is important in terms of specific objectives* you have for yourself. You must edit your writing accordingly.

One final word: "Critical incident" in journal keeping, like any sort of writing, can be useless, a piece of junk, and an unpleasant chore to produce; or it can be an exciting record of your work and a dynamic and useful exploration of yourself. The difference has a lot to do with your attitude toward writing it and the commitment you make to share yourself and your thoughts and feelings about your experience. Only in this way will it become a useful tool for reflection and conceptualization. If you find this writing becoming burdensome or overly difficult and you feel like you are approaching it energetically, ask for help from another intern or your placement or faculty sponsor. After a couple of weeks' practice, this kind of writing should come easy to you and it will form an excellent documentation of your progress during your internship.

Learn from the People, Events, and World Around You

Setting learning objectives and monitoring them through journal keeping is an extremely important element in insuring the learning part of the internship equation. However, since these techniques are so focused on you and your interests, your learning will be incomplete unless you find ways to become aware of the people, events, problems and environment which surround you and your internship, but which do not necessarily impact on you in the most important and direct way.

You may also need to learn more about and from these people and events, not only to insure the learning aspect of your internship but to assist you in your working responsibilities. Solving problems, completing projects, gathering data, etc., may be difficult unless you learn to navigate the often murky waters of your internship organization and investigate it from several different perspectives.

There is no set or easy formula for learning these things. You may be surprised by the difficulty of this aspect of your internship; you may have assumed that, if you keep your ears and eyes open, information will come to you. Our experience as interns or people working with interns is different.

We observe students who have learned so well how to assimilate knowledge from classroom lectures, books and libraries become stupefied when confronted with the need to assume the role of investigative reporter in an agency in order to find out how it operates, or the role of participant-observer in trying to sort out fact from fancy in a particular and complicated experience on the job. Having to search out information to solve a problem or interview co-workers in order to get an answer is a new and sometimes anxiety-ridden experience for many students; and, although there is no simple formula for learning in this way, we offer the following tips:

- Without a set curriculum and an instructor to rely on, you will have to activate yourself in deciding what it is you wish to learn and the best means for learning it. If you have a tendency to sit back and follow other people, particularly in new situations, this aspect of internship learning may be a challenge for you and you may need to push yourself.

- Remember that people love to talk, particularly about themselves, their work, their families, etc. When you are curious about someone or something, don't be afraid to ask. Most people will appreciate and value your interest. They also know you are an intern and, thus, that you are there to learn. Many people — many more than you expect — love to teach.

- As often as we stress objectives and sticking to them, we also have to caution you not to focus on them to such an extent that you become too closed or rigid in relation to your total experience. Be open to the fact that you may wish to add new objectives or change old ones as you go along. Watch out for serendipitous events or experiences which don't seem to fit anywhere in your scheme of things but impact on you or open your eyes in some new way.

Try yourself out in the following experience analysis assignments:

Learn from Your Internship Organization*

The people, events and issues running rampant in your internship organization often comprise an unlimited curriculum in social science, organizational development, politics and the humanities. Here are some aspects relevant to most organizations, including the one you are working in which may attract your interest and some techniques for sorting it all out.

First Impressions

When you first arrive at your internship, write down and catalog your first impressions of the place and the people. While the setting is still new and strange, you will be able to see your surroundings with a certain freshness that will disappear as you settle into the work routine and become less of an outsider. Questions and hunches which you develop early in your in-

---

*These assignments are adapted from "Fieldwork Analysis Reports," Field Study Office, New York State College of Human Ecology, Cornell University, Ithaca, New York 14853.

ternship (e.g., "I wonder why there are so many meetings?" or "It looks like people that have the most clout around here always have corner offices.") are the ones that really help make sense of the organization later on.

Here are some questions to help you organize your impressions:

The Organizational Setting — physical appearance, structure, personnel, clients/ customers:

- What does your organization look like? Your office? Where is it located?
- How do you feel when you are there?
- In general, what does your organization and your section of it do?
- How does your section of the organization fit into the total organization?
- How long has your organization and your section been in existence?
- How large is your organization and your section of it?
- What kind of financial resources does your section of the organization have?
- What are the backgrounds (e.g., race, sex, education) and job responsibilities of the people whom you will be working with?

     What do these people do? How do they dress? Act? Talk?

- Are there any recent changes that your organization and section are responding to (e.g., new leadership, loss of income)?
- Who are the clients/customers of your organization?

     Are they visible? What do they look like? What do they act like?

Your Job:

- What are your job responsibilities?
- How do the responsibilities fit into the activities of your section?
- How do the job responsibilities fit/match your own personal objectives?
- How are you feeling about it?

Your Organization's Goals

Some organizations have clear, specific goals and objectives for their work and others do not. Usually there are some reasons for both situations. Goals can serve as useful mottos to justify the organization's existence to the outside world. They can also serve to obfuscate the real intentions of those that manage or work in an organization.

Sometimes workers don't even know what their organization's goals are. To complicate matters further, some argue that, while the stated goals of welfare programs, for example, are to place an income floor under poor people, the real intent (or at least function) of welfare is to control the amount of unskilled labor that enters the work force while simultaneously keeping a lid on the discontent of the poor.

What are the goals of your organization? Is there consensus or disagreement on them? How were they arrived at? Do they reflect actual practice?

To find out answers to these questions, not only will you have to talk to people in the organization, you may also have to read public relations material, enabling legislation, stockholders' pamphlets, etc. In short, although most organizations are entirely open about their objectives and are willing and eager to discuss them, you may have to investigate further by asking questions of individuals. If you find yourself curious about something, follow up on it.

The Organizational Environment — Internal

Here are some other organizational aspects that may interest you and help you sort out what is going on around you:

People

- Who works in your placement organization?

  What are their backgrounds, education, or other qualifications for the job?
- What are the salaries?

  Are people content or not? Why?

Structure

- How is your placement organized? Who has the influence over whom? Why? How?

Decision making

- What are the major decision-making structure and bodies in your placement organization?
- How autocratic or democratic is it?
- How well does it function?

Leadership

- Who are the leaders in your organization? Who makes things happen?
- Are these people also the bosses? Or, is there a particular secretary or clerk who seems awfully powerful to you? Why? How is he/she influential?

Processing of Information

- How is information processed in your organization?
- How do people find out what they need to know in order to make decisions?

Funding/Budget

- Where does the money come from to operate your organization?
- Look at some operating budgets for your unit or for the organization as a whole. Do you understand them? If not, get someone to help you.
- What are the financial needs of your setting? The outlook?

Your Supervisor

- What motivates him/her? What is he/she aiming for?
- What sort of supervisory style does he/she use with you? Other workers?

Form some notions about these and other questions and check them out with your supervisor. Most likely, he or she will be delighted to talk to you about them. If you sense this sort of conversation would be difficult in your office, take your supervisor to lunch!

The Organizational Environment — External

Look outside your organization. With what other organizations does it interact? How? Which ones does it compete with, cooperate with? If you don't know, find out.

Evaluate Your Organization

After you have been on the job for a while, assess the *efficiency and effectiveness* of your organization. After monitoring and evaluating yourself, it could be fun to change the focus and evaluate your organization. Use its objectives or goals and share your findings with your supervisor, co-workers, other interns. Remember that you probably don't have the whole picture yet, but observing your feelings about these issues can help you sharpen your thinking and learn a great deal about the people you work with.

The Social and Physical Environment of Your Internship: You're a Tourist, Too . . .

If this is not your hometown, then go out and explore. Every place has highlights that should not be missed. With a travel brochure and a map, visit the landmarks, museums, galleries, etc. Experiment with new ways to commute to work on a Saturday and get to know the city "beyond your bus stop." Meeting people and experiencing the city adds to your intern experience. Make the local visitor's center your first stop and don't remain a stranger to a city you work and live in. As you get to know your new home, think about how it affects your work setting and the people there.

Careers — Someday I'd Like To Be . . .

As an intern, you have access to information and people who may not be available to you at any other time. The opportunities are there for you to observe and discover new developments in a particular field, initiate your own research into a new direction or test established academic theories. You have access to hundreds of people in different occupations to whom you can talk and from whom you can learn.

Take this chance to explore and consider diverse careers and organizations. Check out careers in related fields and variations on your old career choices. A professional career in psychology may have lost its appeal; but, after a little research, you may find out that a psychology major can fit very nicely into a public relations career. Your attitudes, interests and goals are all subject to change as you experience your internship. You will become better prepared to make the important career decisions in your life if you use this opportunity to explore your feelings and inclinations, as well as the opportunities and occupations which exist out in the world. Remember, everyone knows you are on an internship to learn as well as to work. Don't be shy about talking to people about anything. If you are up on your work, ask your supervisor for an hour or two off so you can go across town and observe and talk to another intern or worker in a different setting. This is your best and perhaps only chance to find out!

What Do You Say?*

There are no set questions to ask. The best way to determine what to ask is to decide what you want to know when you walk out the door. Once you have decided, then the questions should become obvious. It usually helps to have more questions than can possibly be answered during the interview. Rank them so that you ask the most important questions first. Here are a few samples:

- How did you become interested in this field and start in it?
- How can someone pursue this interest?
- What training or education did you have? Where did you get it?
- How would you do it differently?
- What are your major responsibilities?
- What do you like most about your work? Least?
- What is your schedule?
- What skills do you use most often?
- Is there much pressure in your position?
- How is your performance evaluated?
- What are the major problems, frustrations and difficulties?
- What do you see in the future for this line of work?
- What are some of your other interests which you might pursue?
- What advice would you give to a person interested in this field?
- Who else is going exciting things in this field?

Some questions you might ask about a particular job or occupation —

- What will I need to enter?
- What training is available?
- Are any particular aptitudes needed?
- What personal qualities are useful?
- What limits will the job pose on my free time?
- Will it affect my lifestyle off the job?
- What particular tasks will I have to do?
- Can I specialize in this job?

---

* Contributed by the Office of Career Development and Placement, College of Charleston, Charleston, South Carolina 29401

→ How much responsibility would I be given?

→ What would be my relationship with the boss?

→ Would I be working alone or with others? How many?

→ Would my co-workers be my age or older — or younger?

→ Would all my co-workers be the same sex?

→ Would I be dealing with customers, clients or patients?

→ Would I meet new people constantly?

When pursuing a specific target, you might try these questions:

→ What do you consider ideal experience for this job?

→ Was the previous incumbent promoted?

→ Could you tell me about the people who would be reporting to me?

→ What is the largest single problem facing your staff now?

→ What have been some of the best results produced by people in this job?

→ Could you tell me about the primary people I would be dealing with?

→ What are the primary results you would like to see me produce?

→ May I talk with the person who last held this job? Other members of the staff?

→ How do you see the firm changing in the next five years? Ten years?

Chapter Four

REFLECTIONS ON AN INTERNSHIP — SUMMING IT UP

"Let me read with open eyes the book my days are writing — and learn."

Dag Hammarskjold

The end of an internship is not the end of your learning experience. Through self-evaluation, you can learn how you and others have grown from sharing this learning opportunity and how to use what you have gained. Although there are many ways to sum up and document an internship, we offer a simple but useful technique:

First, obtain feedback on your *work performance* in your internship. Many programs have designed forms for this purpose and faculty sponsors will ask you and/or your placement supervisor to fill one out. Be sure you know whether your placement supervisor must complete such a form and ask to see what he/she writes before the form is sent back to your campus. If your internship program or faculty sponsor do not require such a process, consider using the sample evaluation form that follows to obtain your supervisor's observation on your performance. Look carefully at what he/she writes and discuss any points you do not understand, feel need more clarity, or disagree with.

Sample Evaluation Form

EVALUATION CRITERIA for FIELD PERFORMANCE*

Student:_____   Supervisor: _____

Placement: _____   Date: _____

Directions: The following checklist should assist you in evaluating your student's performance during this term. We are interested in relative growth — relative to where the student started — rather than an absolute measure. Therefore, for each item appropriate or applicable to *your* student in *your* setting, think back to a beginning rating and then indicate the measure of progress that may have been made since then on each of the items listed. Finally, please check those items which represented a particularly difficult struggle for your student.

Not applicable	Poor	Below average	Average	Very good	Outstanding		Not applicable	Became worse	Slacked off some	Stayed the same	Some progress	Greatly improved	Student struggled hard with this one
						Work Habits and Presentation of Self							
						Is punctual and dependable							
						Conforms to expected organization norms							
						Is self-reliant (as appropriate)							
						Looks for new responsibilities, takes initiative...............							
						Dresses neatly and appropriately							
						Has a pleasant, positive demeanor; appears confident, informed and attentive to others							
						Other (please specify) _____							
						Skills in Task Performance							
						Completes assigned tasks							
						Attends to details							
						Manages time and energy well							

* Reprinted with permission: Field Study Office, New York State College of Human Ecology, Cornell University, Ithaca, N.Y. 14853. T. Stanton, Director.

Not applicable	Poor	Below average	Average	Very good	Outstanding		Not applicable	Became Worse	Slacked off some	Stayed the same	Some progress	Greatly improved	Student struggled hard with this one
						Skills in Task Performance (continued)							
						Meets deadlines							
						Understands and follows instructions .							
						Shows judgment about when to seek further guidance, when to be self-reliant							
						Demonstrates specific skills necessary to the job, e.g. writing, research, observation, recording, graphic skills . . .							
						Other skills (please specify) ________ ________________________							
						Attitudes							
						Demonstrates active desire to learn from and contribute to placement organization							
						Has open mind; does not rush to judgment							
						Accepts and makes positive use of criticism							
						Understands and accepts necessity of some dull or repetitive tasks							
						Demonstrates problem solving orientation; looks for positives in difficult situations; looks upon problems as challenges							
						Is inquisitive							
						Has respect for other people's different skills and life experiences							
						Recognizes and accepts own limitations							
						Willing to attempt new challenges . . .							
						Understands difference and strikes balance between roles of worker/student and between organization goals/own goals							

Not applicable	Poor	Below average	Average	Very good	Outstanding		Not applicable	Became Worse	Slacked off some	Stayed the same	Some progress	Greatly improved	Student struggled hard with this one
						Attitudes (continued)							
						Is cooperative, flexible and adaptable .							
						Demonstrates ability to set and refine, then fulfill personal goals							
						Shows openness to self-evaluation . . .							
						Seeks out resources within organization and its affiliates							
						Other (please specify) _____							
						_____							
						Skills in Human Relations							
						Adjusts to a variety of new circumstances, expectations and people							
						Developes new, alternative ways to respond especially when prior expectations are not met							
						Shows ability to question and explore placement organization, its methods, etc., without putting people on the defensive							
						Is sensitive to the needs of others							
						Is a good listener, attentive							
						Copes well with unexpected problems							
						Demonstrates tact							
						Asserts own views and concerns effectively							
						Has tolerance for ambiguity							
						Other (please specify) _____							
						_____							

Growth in Placement

1. What have been the student's major strengths in the placement?

   ....

   ....

   ....

   ....

2. In what areas could the student improve in order to function more effectively
   in the placement?

   ....

   ....

   ....

   ....

3. Did the student develop new skills and knowledge?

   Which ones? ....

   ....

   Did he/she gain new insights into his/her attitudes, behaviors or values?

   Which ones? ....

   ....

   Did he/she discover new interests or aptitudes? ....

   Which ones? ....

   ....

4. How well was this placement suited to the student's abilities and interests?

   ....

   ....

   ....

   ....

   ....

Growth in Placement (continued)

    5.   Did the student make useful contributions? Please describe.

....

....

....

....

....

    6.   Additional comments on your student or on the program:

....

....

....

....

....

....

....

....

....

....

....

....

....

Please return by end of month following student's internship. Thank you.

Second, obtain feedback on the *learning aspects* of your internship:

A.   Once again, go back and *examine your learning objectives* state-
       ment which you wrote back before you started looking for an in-
       ternship and which, hopefully, you refined once you had obtained
       the internship (in a learning contract?) and perhaps refined a week
       or two into the internship.

B.   *Read over your journal* so that you can remember how you pro-
       gressed during the internship.

C.   For each objective you had, *write an evaluation* describing the
       aspects of your internship which relate to that objective and the
       progress you made toward it.

   Example:

   Objective: To learn how nutrition research is used in formulating
   public policy.

   Evaluation: By keeping track of H.R. 831, by attending hearings and
   working with and talking to legislative staff and officials in the Food
   and Nutrition Service, I gained a much clearer insight into how the
   economic needs of food companies and farmers, and the nutrition concerns of policy officials, researchers and consumers interact to create
   public legislation. For instance . . .

   Based on this learning, I find myself wondering . . .

   Example:

   Objective: To learn how to work with people with more sensitivity and
   skill.

   Evaluation: In my internship, I was responsible for interviewing dis-
   abled veterans and referring them to appropriate services. I found it
   very difficult to talk with them at first, particularly when dealing with
   people of different socio-economic backgrounds than my own. I learned
   that I tend to assume things about them that may not always be true,
   that I have to listen more closely to what they are saying and that I can
   not really be of much help unless I know what the services are to which
   I am referring them. Although I often felt helpless and out of place in
   this role, I gained a great deal from it in terms of listening skills and
   awareness of political and cultural differences and their impact on
   human service. Although I find myself hearing more questions than
   answers, I learned more about helping people from this experience than
   from any other in my life.

D.   Now that you have evaluated your experience in this way, *make
       an appointment with your supervisor and share these findings with
       him/her.*   Find out where he/she agrees with you and where you
       two have differences. Do the same thing with another intern or
       co-worker who could observe your work. Take their reactions and
       think about them. Do their views about your progress change
       yours in any way?

E.   *Now write up for yourself a summary of your internship* based on this thinking and talking. How do you feel about your growth and learning during the internship? How about your objectives? Were they realistic? Would you change them now? Are you satisfied with your progress?

F.   What are your *general feelings* about the internship? If you have strong feelings about it, whether positive or negative, before or after leaving your internship, consider sharing your feelings.

G.   *Where does this experience leave you?* Lead you? Having summed up and evaluated your internship experience, what does it lead you to want to do next? How has it altered or reinforced your attitudes toward and direction in school? Whether you plan to return to a college or university or find another work experience, it is time to return to the techniques outlined in Step One, Chapter Two, and think through *new objectives* for yourself now that you have had the internship. Most likely your experience has had an extremely strong impact on you; and you should know whether that means redirecting or continuing your education. How and why.

Evaluating an internship experience and thinking through the next steps are difficult tasks but extremely important ones. Whether your campus-based sponsors require you to or not, you really haven't completed an internship until you have completed this final step. A month or two of vacation or university life can be very distracting and tend to lead you away from the important thoughts and feelings you have now. If you don't think them through and write them down now you may have trouble recalling them later.

Whether or not you follow this structured debriefing or evaluative process, here are some criteria and questions to keep in mind as you pack your bags to return home or to school:

Personal

1.   Did you meet your learning objectives?

2.   How have your academic and career goals changed?

3.   What learning opportunities did you discover and take advantage of "on-the-job?"

4.   Do you feel your work contributed to the organization and community? How?

5.   Did you accept responsibility for your decisions and actions?

6.   What impact did this experience have on your personal growth?

7.   What new things did you learn about yourself?

8.   What insights have you gained into the field of your internship?

Work Performance

1. How well did you work under supervision?

2. Rate your independent performance.

3. Did you accomplish your project goals?

4. What prior skills did you use in the internship? List new skills and knowledge acquired.

5. How do your new knowledge and skills tie into past academic work? Future academic work?

6. How did you resolve your problems? Handle disappointments?

7. What approaches did you use on assigned tasks? Would you do them differently now?

8. Were you satisfied with your performance on assignments and projects?

9. How well did you accept constructive suggestions from others?

10. Did you meet deadlines? Use your time efficiently?

11. Rate the overall quality of your work.

12. Did you learn that you are not as good at some things as you thought? What failures did you have and what did they teach you?

The Internship

1. Did the internship meet your personal expectations?

2. Was the organization open to your ideas? Did they use them?

3. How will your new skills and knowledge be useful in other internships? In permanent jobs?

4. Would you like a career in the field of your internship?

5. Did the internship increase your understanding of standard course material in that subject area? How?

6. How did the internship improve your skills in problem-solving and communication?

7. How much time and commitment was involved in the internship?

8. Would you recommend the organization to other students?

9. How could this experience have been improved?

10. What was your greatest accomplishment?

If you are interested in further thoughts and techniques related to learning from experience, we recommend *Field Study: A Sourcebook for Experiential Learning* edited by Lenore Borzak (Sage Publications, 275 South Beverly Drive, Beverly Hills, CA 90212, price $9.95). It contains eighteen articles by students, teachers, administrators and work supervisors which focus on the process of experiential learning — how to prepare for it, how best to profit from it while in the field, and how to learn from further reflection on the experience. Several methods and practical exercises are included.

Then, there is one final, but all important step . . . →   →   →   →

CELEBRATE!

You deserve it. You spent a period as a self-directed, active, responsible intern. You have accomplished things and responded to challenges far more important and far more intense than those most students deal with back on campus. After months of arduous and sometimes anxious work, you deserve a good time . . . Have one!

INDEX

A

Academic advisor, 17
Academic credit, 13, 29-31, 32, 33
Academic interests, 8
Acceptance letter, 32
Adham, J., 36-41
Alumni, 34
American Political Science Association, 15

B

Betts, F., 46, 47
Bolles, R.N., 7
Borzak, L., 83

C

Careers, 72
Career goals, 8
Career Guide to Professional Associations: A Directory of Organizations by Occupational Field, 16
Career services, 16, 34
Classified ads, 35
College of Charleston, Office of Career Development, 73
Commission on Voluntary Service and Action, 15
Complete Job Search Handbook: All the Skills You Need to Get Any Job and Have a Good Time Doing It, 7
Cooperative education, 3, 13, 17
Cornell University, 23, 26, 37, 76
Council on International Educational Exchange, 15
Co-workers, 44, 49, 50
Critical Incident Journal, 66-68

D

DeHaan, R., 46, 47
Directory of Internships, Work Experience Programs and On-the-Job Training Opportunities, 15
Directory of Special Programs for Minority Group Members: Career Information Services, Employment Skills Banks, Financial Aid Sources, 15
Directory of Undergraduate Internships, 14
Directory of Washington Internships, 14
Directory of Public Service Internships for The Graduate, Post-Graduate, and Mid-Career Professional, 14
Discrimination, 50
Duley, J., vii, 66

E

Environmental Intern Program, 15
Evaluation, 57, 65, 75-83
    Criteria, 76
    Form, 76-80
    of Organization, 72-74
Exercises, 7
Experiential learning, 2, 3, 55, 56

F

Faculty sponsor, 17, 29, 30, 33, 50, 56, 58, 60, 63, 78, 80
Fiddler on the roof, 18
Field Experience: Expand Your Options, 15
Field learning, 1
Field study, 3, 13
Field Study: A Sourcebook for Experiential Learning, 83

One last thing. Send us a note telling us how you like or dislike this book now that you have completed your internship. Your comments will help us revise and improve it as we go along. (You may use this page, if you wish. Just write on it, tear it out and send it to us in care of the Publisher.) Thank you.